The Vagus Nerve Collection

Gut Brain Connection & Meditations to Soothe Your Vagus Nerve

Wendy Hayden

SWH Media, LLC

Copyright ©2023 by Wendy Hayden

All rights reserved.

No portion of this book may be reproduced in any form without written permission from the publisher or author, except as permitted by U.S. copyright law.

Contents

1. Introduction — 1
2. The Vagus Nerve — 9
3. The Vagus Nerve and the Gut — 21
4. Is Your Vagus Nerve Healthy? — 27
5. How to Convince Our Vagus Nerve We Are Safe — 39
6. Breathing for your vagus nerve — 51
7. Cold Exposure to Stimulate Your Vagus Nerve — 71
8. Meditation and prayer — 81
9. EFT, Emotional Freedom Technique or Tapping and the Vagus Nerve — 93
10. Nutrition for Vagal Nerve Health — 103
11. How to Stimulate Your Child's Vagus Nerve — 113
12. Book 2 Meditations to Soothe the Vagus Neve — 121
13. Meditation and Your Vagus Nerve — 123
14. How to Implement a Meditation Practice into Your Daily Routine — 127

15.	Meditation to Stimulate the Vagus Nerve	131
16.	Meditation to Calm Your Vagus Nerve	135
17.	Meditation to Get Out of Fight or Flight	139
18.	Meditation to Calm Your Nervous System	143
19.	Meditation to Improve Digestion	147
20.	Meditation to Release Anxiety	151
21.	Meditation to Release Anger	155
22.	Meditation to Release Fear	159
23.	Meditation to Release Resentment	163
24.	Meditation for Deep Sleep	167
25.	Meditation for an Inner Sense of Connection and Belonging	171
26.	Meditation to Reduce Inflammation	175
27.	Meditation for Healing and Peace	179
28.	Meditation for Autoimmune Disease	183
29.	Meditation for PTSD	187
30.	Meditation for IBS	191
31.	Meditation for Constipation Relief	195
32.	Meditation to Help Your Child Get Out of Fight or Flight	199
33.	Meditation to Feel Safe	203
34.	Meditation for Connection	207

| 35. | Meditation for Pain Relief | 211 |
| 36. | Make Meditation a Long Term Part of Healing Your Vagus Nerve | 215 |

Chapter 1

Introduction

I have been on a quest to heal my family's health for the better part of the last decade. My husband has Crohn's disease and had his large intestines and colon removed before I met him. My youngest son was diagnosed with autism, celiac, Tourette's, anxiety and struggled with chronic constipation. My oldest son has Asthma. My two sons and I have been diagnosed with PTSD. In my extended family, there are multiple diagnoses, including Rheumatoid Arthritis, depression, type 2 diabetes, and IBS.

At 16 months old, my youngest son was hospitalized for 5 days with Salmonella. Doctors put him on IV antibiotics. They saved his life but set off terrible gut issues. At 18 months, his pediatrician diagnosed him with Celiac disease. At 4 years old, he was again hospitalized. This time for rotavirus. His pediatric gastroenterologist prescribed Miralax. I was told that he'd need to be on it for life. My son's mental health took a nosedive during the year and a half. He was on Miralax. He developed anxiety, panic attacks, and hallucinations. A pediatric neurologist diagnosed him with Tourrettes's syndrome,

PDD-nos, and later Autism. Every doctor I talked to assured me that Miralax wasn't causing these issues and told me I had to keep giving it to him.

Then my husband had surgery to repair a bladder fistula. The surgery went wrong and almost killed him. After this surgery, he was in the hospital for 6 weeks and on TPN nutrition for 6 months. His surgeon told him he should go on permanent disability.

I read everything I could and tried everything I learned to heal my family. We changed our diet and used supplements I read about. We found an integrative medicine doctor who worked with us to help us heal. My family made great strides, and I learned so much.

I made it my mission to heal my family. I made bone broth, fermented foods and cooked with veggies we grew in our garden. I served my family home-cooked organic food and read the label on every item I bought at the store.

My husband got off steroids and immune suppressors. He bought his own business where he worked 6 days a week, 60-hour weeks. He was tired, but he looked wonderful and was healthier than he had been his entire adult life. We knew we could never get him in perfect health because of the surgical damage and not having large intestines, but he was feeling better than he had since he was 12 and developed Inflammatory Bowel Disease and his doctor put him on steroids and immune suppressors.

INTRODUCTION

I got my son off of Miralax and healed the damage it did to him. I worked to heal his gut and as it healed; he flourished. As his gut health improved, his mental health improved, too. He stopped ticcing; he went from hardly talking to doing public speaking at living history events. His anxiety melted away. He started hitting every age-appropriate milestone and even exceeding them. He grew like a weed.

I used what I had learned to help thousands of families with children who were struggling with chronic constipation, both through my Facebook groups and with my books, 'What Your Doctor Didn't Tell You About Childhood Constipation' and 'End You Chronic Constipation, Now!' and my children's books.

I felt like I really had figured it all out.

Then my husband's health started going downhill again. The stress of running a business slowly ate away at my husband's physical and mental health. For the first time in years, he had a Crohn's flare. He kept getting blockages from the scar tissue in his intestines and was having pain from his Crohn's disease. He began having a horrible urgency that made it hard for us to leave the house and sometimes could not make it to work without having to stop at a gas station for a restroom break.

We ended up back at our Integrative Medicine Doctor. He told my husband that the stress of running the business would kill him and that we needed to make big changes. Our doctor told us that stress and trauma were causing my husband's flare and that until we got rid of the stress and get to the root of the trauma that had triggered his autoimmune disease in the first place or his health would not get better. It was a big switch in thinking for us.

Our doctor told us that trauma can damage our DNA, causing the disease to be passed down through the generations. Since many of my husband's family members have autoimmune issues, this made a ton of sense to us. He also told us it didn't matter how healthy we eat or how careful we were with our gut health, or what supplements we took; if we had unresolved trauma, nothing we did would work to heal our bodies long term.

I knew from my interest in DNA that just because you have a gene for a disease; it doesn't mean that you will get the disease. You can just be a carrier of a gene for Crohn's or Celiac. Something needs to trigger your DNA to cause that gene to express itself.

We weren't in a position to sell his business or just throw the keys on the desk and walk away, so I researched ways to help him deal with the daily stress he was experiencing and also began looking into trauma and how it triggers the autoimmune disease.

I dove deep, reading books, articles and watching hours and hours of videos.

INTRODUCTION

My "Aha!" moment came watching a talk by Dr. Stephen Porges. Dr. Porges is the pioneer researcher behind the Polyvagal theory. As he talked about the vagus nerve and its impact on so many health issues, I realized this might be the key to healing my family long-term and that this information could also help my readers who struggle with constipation, autoimmune diseases, and gut dysfunction.

I am not a scientist or a doctor. I am a wife, a mom, and a human who is trying to take what I learn and use it to heal myself and my family, and my community.

The health issues my family has had have pushed me to learn more about the standard medical model and effective natural alternatives to the toxic and ineffective treatments prescribed to my family.

I wrote this book to share what I have learned with you. The techniques I have included in this book are ones you can easily implement into your daily life. They will help you heal yourself and heal your family.

There are some wonderful books written by scientists, including "The Polyvagal Theory" by Dr. Stephen Porges, if you are looking for a thorough analysis of the science behind the vagus nerve.

This book will give you an understanding of what the vagus nerve is and how it affects your health, but I am a layperson writing for laypeople. It lays out techniques to help you hack your autonomic nervous system, get out of fight-or-flight mode, and tap into the healing power of the vagus nerve.

As I wrote each chapter of this book, it stirred my emotions up. Past trauma of my own, and of my loved ones, bubbled up. Things that I have tried to avoid thinking about called out for me to not ignore them but to work through them. I had to take breaks from writing when the emotions got to be too much. If you need to take breaks while working on healing your vagus nerve, that is fine. Go at the pace comfortable to you.

Feeling safe is the most important part of this healing journey. If anything in the book makes you feel unsafe, you can skip it and come back to it later when you are ready, or just skip it completely. There is no right or wrong way to go through the chapters in the book or through your healing process.

Some techniques outlined in this book clicked for me and felt comfortable, and some made me feel anxious. If any make you feel increased anxiety or discomfort, move on to another technique.

One wonderful thing about the vagus nerve is that there are a lot of ways to stimulate it. If you notice an increase in gut symptoms while doing any of the techniques outlined in this book, stop and try to figure out what is causing the symptoms. Are you feeling an increase in anxiety? Have you had stressful memories pop up? Are you feeling stressed out from trying to implement too many techniques at once?

Once you figure out what is going on, you can develop a program that works for you and helps you to improve your gut and your mental health.

INTRODUCTION

We all have trauma, tragedies, illness, and stressors, big and small, that cause damage, but with the right tools, you can heal and thrive. I hope this book gives you the tools you need to heal and get your gut and your family's guts functioning optimally.

If you feel overwhelmed at any point while reading this book, please reach out to a therapist, psychologist, or other practitioners who can support you through your journey to healing and wellness.

Chapter 2

The Vagus Nerve

The vagus nerve is the longest cranial nerve in our body and connects our brain to all of our major organs. It is the gut-brain connection. The vagus nerve allows the brain to send and receive messages from our facial muscles, throat, heart, lungs, and digestive tract. Signals travel in both directions along the vagus nerve. 80% of the signals travel to the brain from the organs in the body.

When we talk about the mind-body connection or the gut-brain connection, we are talking about the vagus nerve. The vagus nerve runs from the hypothalamus area of your brain through your chest, wraps around your heart and solar plexus, diaphragm, and to your intestines.

The vagus nerve is the care-taking nerve in our body, sending and receiving signals that help us feel safe and loved.

Compassion and kindness from others, and towards ourselves, stimulates the vagus nerve. Even petting our cat or dog can stimulate the vagus nerve. When we feel love for others, for ourselves, or for our pets, our vagus nerve is stimulated and signals for the release of the feel-good hormone, oxytocin.

There are 12 cranial nerves in our body. They are present in pairs and link the brain with other parts of the body. Some carry sensory information, including details about smells, sights, tastes, and sounds, to the brain. These nerves are identified as having sensory functions. Other cranial nerves regulate the movement of various muscles and the function of certain glands. These are recognized as motor functions.

Some cranial nerves perform either sensory or motor functions, others have both. The vagus nerve performs both sensory and motor functions. Cranial nerves are numbered using Roman counting based on their location. The vagus nerve is also known as nerve X.

Sensory functions of the vagus nerve are as follows;

- Producing somatic sensation information for the skin behind the ear, the external part of the ear canal, and specific parts of the throat

- Providing visceral sensation information for the larynx, esophagus, lungs, trachea, heart, and most of the digestive tract

- Performing a minor role in the sensation of taste near the root of the tongue.

Motor functions of the vagus nerve involve:

- Stimulating the muscles present in the pharynx, larynx, and the soft palate, which is the fleshy area near the back of the roof of the mouth.

- Stimulating muscles in the heart, where it assists to lower resting heart rate.

Stimulating involuntary contractions in the digestive tract, including the esophagus, stomach, and most of the intestines, which enable food to move through the tract.

The vagus nerve sends powerful signals to our brain. We even use language that shows how our nerves are sending us powerful signals. Someone "gets on our nerves" or we have a "gut feeling."

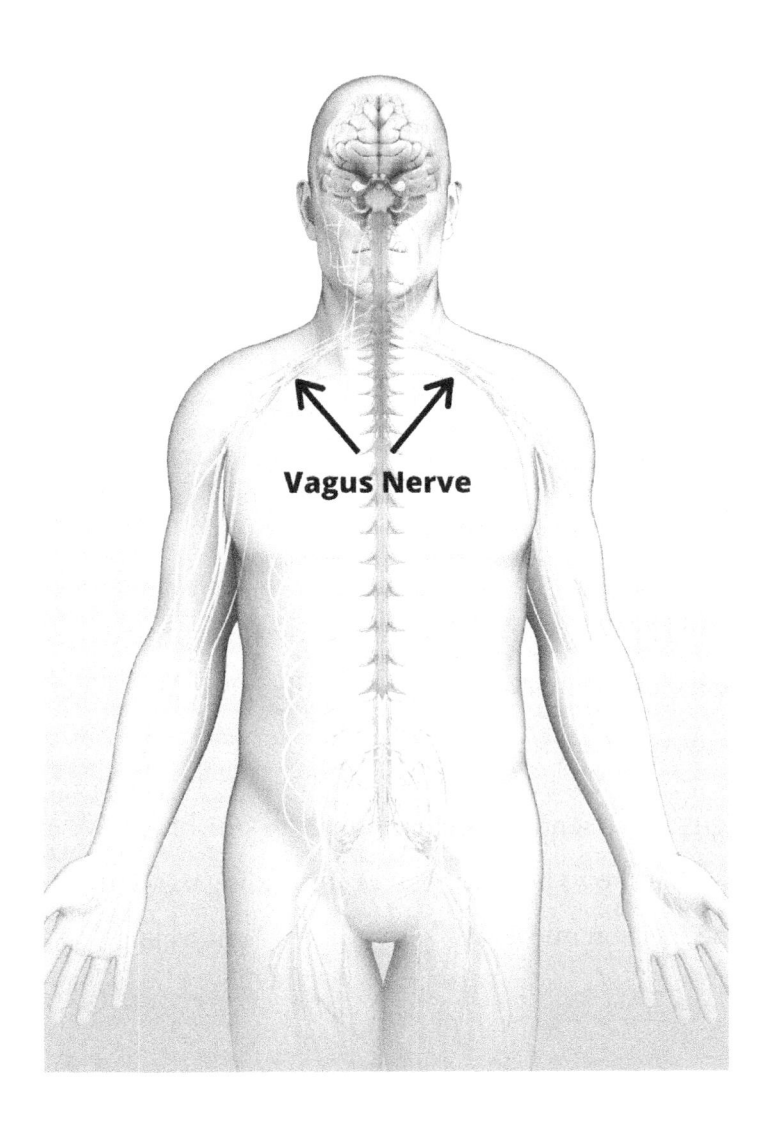

THE VAGUS NERVE

The vagus nerve controls the parasympathetic nervous system.

The parasympathetic nervous system is part of the autonomic nervous system. The autonomic nervous system regulates our automatic or unconscious actions such as our heart beating, the digestion of our food, blood pressure, body temperature, our metabolism, sexual response, or breathing.

The parasympathetic nervous system handles the "rest and digest" or "feed and breed" activities. The parasympathetic nervous system works with the sympathetic nervous system.

The sympathetic nervous system handles our fight, flight, freeze reactions. These two nervous systems work in opposition to each other. When one is turned on, it turns the other off. Your body can't be in a parasympathetic state while it is in a sympathetic state. If you are in a stressed state, your body can not heal, rest, or digest your food properly.

When we are in a sympathetic state for a lengthy period, our vagus nerve weakens or loses tone. Vagal tone is basically how healthy our vagus nerve is. The higher our vagal tone, the easier it is for us to switch into a relaxed, rest and digest state.

The autonomic nervous system's job is to keep us alive. It prioritizes stress over all other systems, including the digestive and immune. It decides where to put our energy and resources.

If we are in a life-threatening situation, our autonomic nervous system shuts down our parasympathetic nervous system and puts all of our energy into saving our life with our sympathetic nervous system taking the lead.

If we were being chased by a wild animal, our sympathetic nervous system would give our body the signal to fight, run or freeze, depending on what would be the most beneficial to us in that situation.

A body stuck in the sympathetic fight-or-flight response can not heal.

The problem with modern living is that our autonomic nervous system has a tough time telling the difference between a physical threat and an emotional threat. A real tiger or a "paper tiger" chasing us.

If you have ever watched a scary movie or TV show and felt your heart race listening to a scary soundtrack, or held your breath in fear at a fictional event taking place on the screen, it will make sense to you that our nervous system has a hard time telling what is real from what is imaginary. Nothing bad was happening to you, but your body isn't able to tell the difference between reality and illusion. Our brain signaled our heart or our lungs that we were in danger. That signal was sent down the vagus nerve to those organs, causing our hearts to race or us to hold our breath waiting for the bad guy to jump out on screen.

It sets our autonomic nervous system up to err on the side of caution and protects us from danger to keep us alive. The autonomic nervous system decides where to put resources and energy. If the scary movie was real, it would make sense for our hearts to pump to give us more blood to outrun the danger or for us to hold our breath to be quiet and not heard by a stalking animal.

If we were in a life-or-death struggle with a bad guy or a wild animal, it wouldn't make sense for us to stop and have sex or have a bowel movement.

We could be killed.

Our autonomic nervous system prioritizes things that will help us escape danger so we can live. Can we make friends or do we need to fight or run?

It is natural for us to switch back and forth between sympathetic and parasympathetic states.

A car veers into our lane, almost hitting our car, and our sympathetic response helps to keep us safe. Our heart beats quicker, sending blood to our brain, helping us to think quickly to avoid getting hit. After we avoid the accident, our body is supposed to switch back into a parasympathetic state.

Unfortunately, that doesn't always happen as it should. Especially when we are in a long-term stressful situation.

When we are stressed because of work, school, family relationships, or trauma, our autonomic nervous system can put us in a fight, flight, or freeze mode for an extended period.

While a stressful job or a toxic relationship will not kill us immediately, our autonomic nervous system can't tell the difference between an actual physical threat to our lives and an emotional threat.

Besides stress, pathogens, bacteria, parasites or diseases can also attack our vagus nerve. Because our vagus nerve protects us, invaders can target it.

A myelin sheath covers the vagus nerve. This myelin sheath protects the nerve. When it is damaged, the nerve won't work as it should and it loses tone.

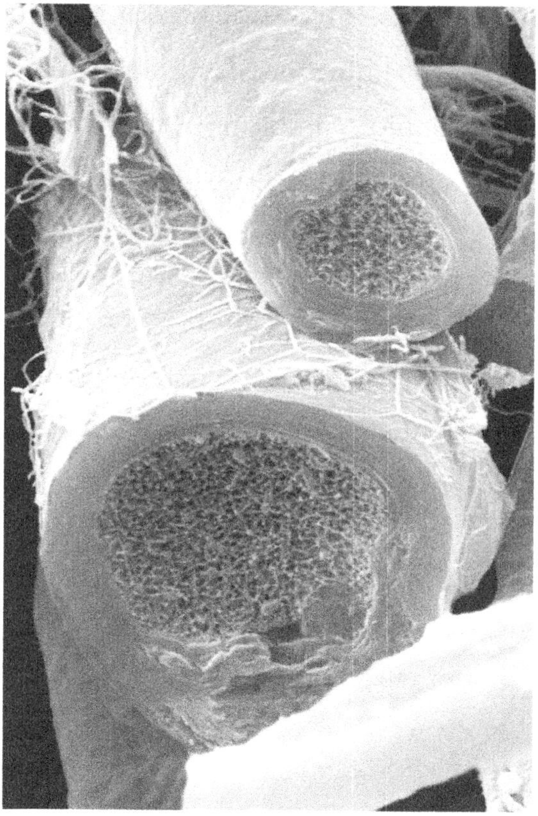

When our vagus nerve loses tone, we can develop issues such as autoimmune diseases, inflammation, depression, anxiety, heart palpitations, headaches, tinnitus, problems swallowing, fatigue, seizures, blood pressure issues, autism, constipation, weight issues, autoimmune disease, leaky gut, and IBS symptoms.

The reason so many distinct problems can be caused by the vagus nerve is that the vagus nerve is connected to so many organs in our body. When it isn't functioning properly, we can experience symptoms in many systems of our body.

The vagus nerve is named after the Latin word vagus, which means wandering. The vagus nerve "wanders" from our brain to just about every major organ in our body. Because it is connected to so many organs in our body, when it isn't functioning properly, there are many repercussions.

Before I researched the vagus nerve, I did not know that our nervous system had anything to do with autoimmune disease. Since autoimmune disease riddles my family, it was very interesting to me when I learned about this connection. It has never made sense to me that our body would attack itself.

The vagus nerve directly detects foreign intruders, parasites, pathogens, mold, spores, chemical toxins, parasites, bacteria, infections, and blood-borne illnesses. The vagus nerve detects something bad and signals the body to send in inflammatory cytokines to destroy the foreign intruder.

If the vagus nerve is damaged or has "low tone", then it can't turn off the cytokines. The cytokines then accidentally attack friendly host cells (your cells and neurons) causing an autoimmune disorder.

The vagus nerve is trying to protect you.

The infection attacks the vagus nerve to keep it from protecting you. It infects the vagus nerve, weakening the nerve fibers and making it less effective. This causes autoimmune issues.

Early in my research, I came across a clinical trial titled "Vagus nerve stimulation inhibits cytokine production and attenuates disease severity in rheumatoid arthritis" [1] published in "Proceedings of the National Academy of Sciences (PNAS)." The trial showed that "stimulating the vagus nerve with an implantable bioelectronic device significantly improved measures of disease activity in patients with rheumatoid arthritis (RA)." I have a close family member with RA, so this grabbed my interest.

The VNS device used in the trial is a bioelectric medical device that uses pulses of electricity to treat diseases. They implanted an electrode on the left cervical vagus nerve in the patient's chest. Slight pulses of electricity stimulated the vagus nerve. There was a reduction in "tumor necrosis factor (TNF), an inflammatory molecule that is a major therapeutic target in RA" when the VNS device was used to stimulate the vagus nerve.

---

1. . https://pubmed.ncbi.nlm.nih.gov/27382171/

The findings of the study showed that active electrical stimulation of the vagus nerve lessened the severity of RA in a majority of the study participants with no serious side effects. But implanting a VNS device is very invasive and expensive.

Thankfully, in my research, I have found many ways to increase your vagus nerve tone that are free, easy, and not invasive.

Chapter 3

The Vagus Nerve and the Gut

The vagus nerve is the Gut-Brain connection. We hear about the gut-brain connection all the time, but what the actual connection is, isn't discussed often. The vagus nerve is the highway that travels from the gut to the brain. Messages travel from the gut to the brain and from the brain to the gut along the Vagus nerve. Most of the communication is from the gut telling the brain what it needs to work properly. 80-90% of the communication messages are from the gut traveling up to the brain.

Your vagus nerve must function to have a bowel movement.

We start digestion even before our food crosses our lips. Thinking about food or smelling food triggers our autonomic system to send digestive juices to our gut, preparing our body to digest our food. Our vagus nerve is sending signals from our brain to our digestive system that food is coming and that our body needs to prepare for digestion.

To show this, imagine a lemon. Think about cutting into that lemon and then taking a slice of the lemon and putting it in your mouth. Imagine sucking all the juice out of that sour lemon.

Chances are your mouth watered, just thinking about that lemon.

If you have a lemon, you can cut it open, smell it, and you will feel your mouth water in anticipation of eating that lemon. Our mind is sending signals through our vagus nerve to ready our digestive system for the imminent arrival of food.

Chewing is critical to digestion. Chewing doesn't just break down food. Enzymes that break down our food fill our saliva. When we chew our food thoroughly, we mix the enzymes into the chewed-up food, starting digestion even before we swallow.

Swallowing is an autonomic function in our body. While we can intentionally swallow, our body swallows automatically, both food and saliva. Our digestive enzymes, and our stomach acid, break down food and also extract nutrients from the food for our body.

Besides digestion, 80% of our immune system is in our gut. Poor gut health, leaky gut, and vagus nerve issues lead to immune problems, including autoimmune diseases.

Food intolerances and nutrient deficiencies, especially vitamin D and glutathione can cause leaky gut; underlying infections like SIBO, yeast, mold, or detox pathways that aren't working efficiently make our body toxic. Chronic stress, trauma, insulin resistance, hormone imbalances, estrogen dominance, adrenal fatigue/cortisol imbalance, and vagus nerve dysfunction can also cause leaky gut.

The lining of our gut is just one cell thick and is the only thing that separates our stool from our blood system. When we get leaky gut, microscopic particles of toxins travel through the wall of our gut into our body, causing inflammation and autoimmune issues. Our body tries to protect us by attacking the toxic molecules.

When the vagus nerve is stimulated, it heals the tight junctions between the cells in the gut.

A recent study done in France[1] with implanted Vagal Nerve Stimulators in Crohn's patients, similar to the study done on RA patients, showed a very positive outcome. After one year, most of the patients went into clinical or endoscopic remission, had restored vagal tone, and saw a reduction in pain and inflammation.

When the vagus nerve isn't working properly, communication between the gut and the brain breaks down and the gut doesn't get what it needs.

Low vagal tone causes constipation, low stomach acid, leaky gut, inflammation in the gut, imbalance in gut bacteria, and a lack of digestive enzymes to break down food. When the vagus nerve isn't working properly, there is a lack of communication between the microbiome to the brain. Lack of communication between the mi-

---

1.. https://onlinelibrary.wiley.com/doi/full/10.1111/nmo.13911

crobiome to the brain causes problems with bacteria, parasites, and yeast.

When we are in fight-or-flight mode, our body makes fewer digestive enzymes. Our body isn't worried about digestion when we are in a state of stress. Our body thinks it needs our energy to be directed at running from what is chasing us, not digesting the food we just ate. When we are chronically stressed, our body doesn't produce as many digestive enzymes, which affects how we digest our food over a lengthy period.

Low vagal tone affects peristalsis. Peristalsis is the wavelike system of contractions of the muscles in the intestines that move the ball of food through the digestive system. Is the food being pushed through the digestive system in the right way at the right rate? When you have a low vagal tone, the food doesn't move through the digestive system properly, leading to a host of problems.

Low stomach acid can lead to many problems. We need stomach acid to digest our food, fight off parasites, stop reflux and fight bad gut bacteria. Many people struggling with reflux think they have too much stomach acid, so they take acid reducers. But a certain level of stomach acid triggers the sphincter muscle that stops reflux. If you lower your stomach acid, the sphincter muscle isn't triggered to close. This leads to reflux. When our vagus nerve isn't working, we don't produce the proper amount of stomach acid, which can lead to reflux. Stomach acid helps break down our food. If you are struggling with constipation or you see undigested food in your stool, you might not have enough stomach acid.

You can eat an organic whole-food diet, fermented foods, probiotics, digestive enzymes, and supplements to heal your gut, but if your vagus nerve isn't working right, you will fight an uphill battle to improve how your gut works. You will still have gut problems if your vagus nerve has a low tone.

We also make GABA and serotonin in our gut. GABA and serotonin are neurotransmitters that impact our mental health. Gut dysfunction can cause depression, anxiety, and other mental health issues.

Prenatal stress or traumatic birth can lead to babies being born with leaky gut, low stomach acid, and low digestive enzymes, causing chronic problems in digestion from birth. Childhood trauma can also lead to chronic gut issues.

The stressor can be physical, or emotional, from toxins, heavy metals, or illness, and it can be a one-time traumatic event or cumulative stress over a long period. Research has shown that trauma is inherited. If your parent or grandparent suffered abuse or trauma, you can inherit that trauma through your DNA.

Chapter 4

Is Your Vagus Nerve Healthy?

Past or current traumas, infections, parasites, chronic stress, chronic illness, toxic relationships, abuse, or neglect can cause problems with our vagus nerve. But anything that makes us feel unsafe can affect the health of our vagus nerve. If students bullied you in school, if you moved frequently and weren't able to be a part of a community, had mold in your home or work environment, if you work in a stressful job or have a stressful home life, it can affect your vagus nerve.

Some signs that your vagus nerve isn't working as it should:

- Swallowing or coughing issues
- Heart palpitations
- High blood pressure
- Shallow breathing, using the chest instead of the belly

- Slow to digest food/undigested food in stool/constipation
- Liver problems
- Acid reflux/Low Stomach Acid/Heartburn/GERD
- OCD
- Migraines
- Poor circulation
- Leaky gut
- Hiatal hernia
- Kidney problems
- Parkinson's Disease
- Gallbladder problems
- Cortisol issues
- Hormone problems, including issues with your menstrual cycle, reproductive organs, or menopause
- Autoimmune diseases
- PTSD
- Depression

- Anxiety

- Migraines

- Seizures

- Inflammation

- Autism

- Sleep issues

- Obesity and weight issues

- Tinnitus

- OCD, ADD, ADHD

- Gastroparesis

- IBS

- Fibromyalgia

- Diabetes

- Sexual dysfunction

- Sleep apnea

If it seems strange that the vagus nerve can cause issues with so many body systems, remember that the nerve is very long and is sending signals back and forth between our brains and almost all of our major organs. So when it isn't functioning correctly, it can affect many organs in our body.

It sends electrical signals to just about every major organ in our body. Our body is almost like a human battery, with the nerves being the wires that transmit energy and signals from the brain to our organs and also from the organs to the brain.

Certain medications like Benadryl, Xanax, some anti-anxiety and antispasmodic drugs, and anticholinergic medications work by blocking acetylcholine, the neurotransmitter of the vagus nerve.

Anticholinergic drugs are used to treat dizziness, peptic ulcers, ulcerative colitis, diverticulitis, cystitis, motion sickness, vertigo, asthma, prostatitis, and COPD, among other issues.

If you have been taking these drugs, your vagus nerve could be impacted negatively.

You can test the health of your vagus nerve in multiple ways.

One way is by testing your gag reflex. If you do not gag, maybe your vagus nerve isn't working well.

IS YOUR VAGUS NERVE HEALTHY?

Another way to test your vagus nerve is to test your bowel transit time. This is a fantastic test to do if you are dealing with constipation, diarrhea, or any gut issues. To do this test, you can use white sesame seeds and track how long it takes for them to pass through your digestive system. If you can't have sesame or can't find white sesame seeds, you can use corn.

Take 1 Tablespoon of white sesame seeds and put them in a glass of water. Drink the water and seeds down without chewing the seeds or corn.

Mark down the time you drink the seeds. Look for the time when you first see the sesame seeds come out. Optimally, the time from when you see the seeds until you no longer see the seeds should be between 16 and 20 hours. Seeing the seeds between 12 and 24 hours is acceptable, but not optimal.

Another test is to test your breathing. You can put one hand on your chest and one hand on your stomach. Take three deep breaths.

1............2..............3..............

Do you feel the breaths in your chest or in your belly? If your hand on your chest is lifting and lowering, it is a sign that you are in a stressed state and can be a sign of vagus nerve dysfunction. If your belly is where you feel your breaths, then that is an excellent sign that you are in a relaxed state.

Heart rate variability (HRV) is an important sign of vagal health. Heart rate variability represents the time difference, or fluctuation, between each heartbeat. Our heart does not beat in exactly the same rhythm with each beat. HRV is thought to be an index of sympathetic to parasympathetic balance of heart rate fluctuation.

There is a correlation between an increase in heart rate variability and lower inflammation. The vagus nerve releases acetylcholine that blocks cytokine production by cells, reducing inflammation.

Heart rate variability is measured by a doctor using an EKG or ECG. Some wearable fitness measurement devices can also monitor HRV.

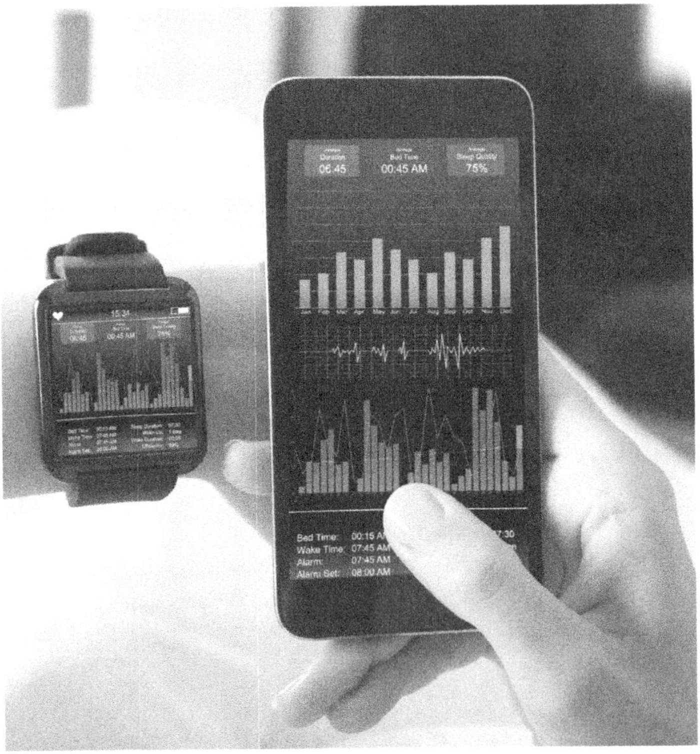
06:45
00:45 AM
75%
Bed Time:
Wake Time 07:45 AM
Alarm: 07:45 AM
Alarm Set: 08:00 AM

Your heart rate is not meant to stay the same all the time. It should vary depending on your physical and emotional state. A high HRV helps you to perform well in stressful situations. If your heart isn't working well, it has the same heart rate whether you are stressed physically or emotionally. Deep breathing can help to improve HRV.

Childhood trauma can affect our physical and mental health long after we grow up. Sexual abuse, physical abuse, emotional abuse, verbal abuse, or neglect by our caretakers when we are young can put us into a state of perpetual fight or flight and cause our body to attack itself.

For our parasympathetic nervous system to function properly, we need to feel safe. If we experienced trauma or abuse as a child, we may never have felt safe.

The ACE (Adverse Childhood Experiences) study by the CDC in 1998 showed a powerful link between childhood trauma and the development of chronic disease and social and emotional problems. Of the 17,000 people surveyed as part of the study, 87% had more than an ACE score of over one.

The ACE study measured 10 distinct types of childhood trauma, including personal trauma and trauma relating to other family members, such as having an alcoholic parent or a parent who was a victim of abuse.

To determine your ACE score, answer the questions in the quiz. For each yes, you add one point to your score. Add up the points at the end to determine your score. The higher your ACE score, the higher your risk for physical and emotional health problems.

The ACE test doesn't include all childhood traumas just the most common ones, so you may have a higher risk for health issues than your ACE score shows if you have suffered other traumas or stressful events that are not included in this test, but the ACE test will give you an idea of the impact of any trauma you have experienced as a child on your health.

Visit to take the ACE test and determine your ACE score.

The higher your ACE score, the higher your risk of chronic diseases, including autoimmune disease, lung cancer, heart disease, depression, and diabetes.

A high ACE score also increases the risk for drug use, suicide, teen pregnancy, and your chances of being a victim or a perpetrator of violence.

A score of 4 or more ACE events has significant ramifications for your health.

According to the website, "The likelihood of chronic pulmonary lung disease increases 390 percent; hepatitis 240 percent; depression 460 percent; attempted suicide 1,220 percent."

There are many other traumas that are not included in the ACE questionnaire that can still lead to vagus nerve dysfunction.

Birth trauma can also cause life-long health issues. If your mother experienced stress during pregnancy, health complications, the death of a family member, a divorce, or anything that affected your mother negatively, this causes birth trauma. Mothers can also experience birth trauma if they have these issues during their pregnancy and the birth of their child.

When a woman is pregnant, she is very vulnerable. She is on high alert and it heightens her senses. This makes her more susceptible to trauma during her pregnancy and birth. This affects the baby through the placenta, transferring the trauma to the baby.

Besides childhood trauma and birth trauma, trauma as an adult can have a big impact on your health. Divorce, the death of a loved one, physical or emotional abuse, legal problems, financial struggles, a loved one being ill, moving, chronic stress, infections, or parasites can trigger health issues.

If the vagus nerve is attacked by an infection or parasite, it can send our immune system into overdrive to destroy the parasite or the infection. When our vagus nerve isn't functioning properly, it doesn't always stop sending these signals of danger, leading our immune system to continue to attack cells even after the parasite or infection is gone. This leads to autoimmunity.

Our vagus nerve is trying to protect us and take care of us but can send signals to our immune system to attack healthy cells.

If we can heal our vagus nerve and get it to work properly, we can stop it from signaling attacks on our body.

Chapter 5

How to Convince Our Vagus Nerve We Are Safe

We must be in parasympathetic nervous system dominance to heal our bodies. If we are in a state of sympathetic nervous system dominance, all of our energy goes toward keeping us alive and safe.

To switch from sympathetic to parasympathetic, we need our vagus nerve to work properly and signal to our brain that we are safe and not in danger.

There are many ways to communicate with our body that we are not in danger. Some are easier than others. Some are within our control, and some are harder for us to control.

If you are in an abusive relationship, you need support leaving that relationship. Please see a therapist for help.

Being aware of how you are reacting to a situation can make a sizable difference in how you feel about the situation.

If you felt yourself slip into fight, flight or freeze mode, it's helpful to ask yourself the following questions:

Am I in physical danger?

Is what I am feeling productive or helpful in this situation?

What reaction can I have that will help me handle this situation better?

Who in my life supports me?

What can I change to make my situation less stressful?

Group situations like a concert, church, or meeting a group of friends for a meal, can have a positive effect on our feelings of safety and peacefulness. Community is very important to our emotional health.

Being with people that support us and that we feel a connection stimulates our vagus nerve.

The vagus nerve signals the release of oxytocin, the bonding, or the love hormone. When we are in church or at a concert or even listening to music in our home, the vagus nerve signals to release oxytocin. This gives us a feeling of peace and turns on our parasympathetic response.

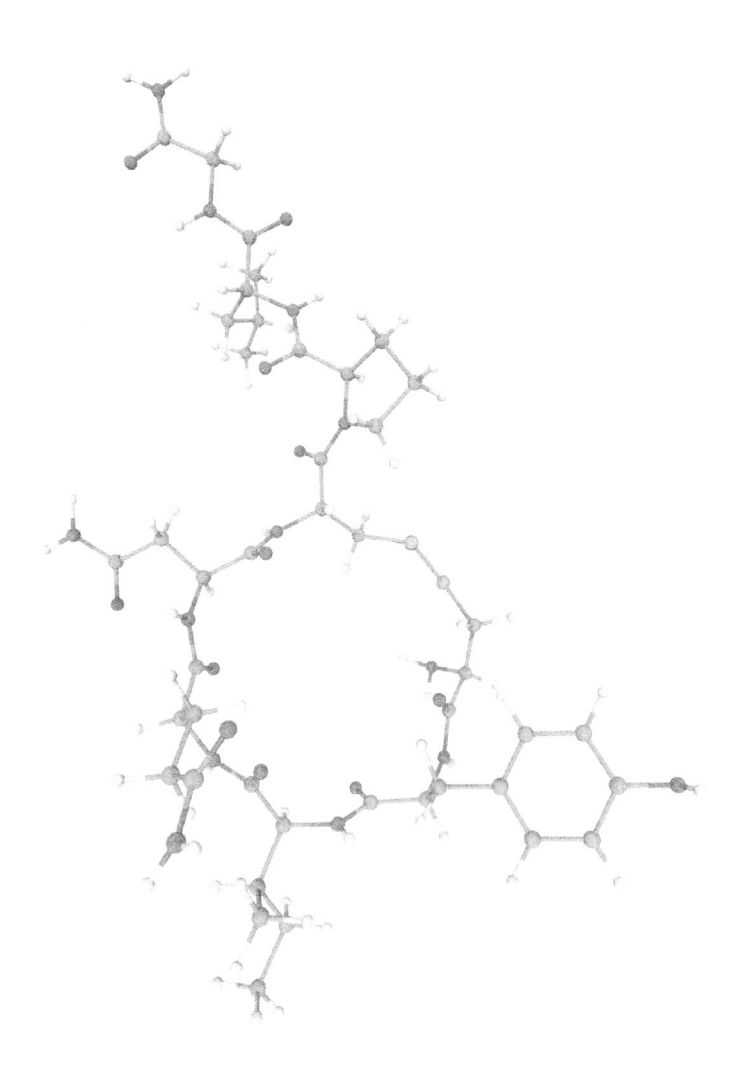

We think of oxytocin as just a hormone that is part of the birthing or breastfeeding process or the hormone that bonds us to our baby, but it involves much more than that. Oxytocin increases feelings of love, empathy, and connection to others and facilitates feelings of trust.

We release oxytocin during sexual activity. It is integral in the formation of pair bonds. Men and women both release oxytocin. It also bonds group members, especially when we feel that the members of the group are like us. Increasing our oxytocin lowers our feelings of fear and has an antidepressant effect. Scientists believe that oxytocin reduces inflammation by decreasing cytokines.

The vagus nerve sends cytokines to destroy invaders, but they cause inflammation. Inflammation protects us short-term. But it can cause problems long-term or when there aren't any foreign invaders but just our own cells attacking our bodies, triggering autoimmune disease.

Turning off inflammation is critical to healing our vagus nerve.

We may not be able to control how stressful certain things are, like having a sick child or being in the middle of a divorce, but we can control how we react to these things. Reframing the situation can help you see things in a different light.

Some examples of reframing are:

My child may be sick, but I have found the best doctors to help my child get better.

Going through this divorce is hard, but it is the first step I am taking toward building a joyful, peaceful life.

My job is very stressful, but it is preparing me for a better position down the road.

I feel overwhelmed, but I am learning so much that I will handle this better in the future.

Changing how you think about a situation can help you move out of a sympathetic response.

Can you list a few of your chief worries and reframe them in a more positive light?

It is important to treat yourself with the same love and compassion with which you treat others.

When we are in a fight, flight, or freeze state, survival mode kicks in and sometimes our brains have us do things we feel shame or regret for doing later on.

Remember, you were doing your best to survive a difficult, dangerous, or traumatic situation and that you did the best you could in that situation.

Having love, compassion, and forgiveness for yourself will help you heal and help your vagus nerve.

HOW TO CONVINCE OUR VAGUS NERVE WE ARE... 45

Surrounding yourself with people who make you feel loved, accepted, and safe is also very important to get out of fight-or-flight mode. Having a community of supportive, loving, and fun friends and family can help you feel safe.

Being a part of a safe group can help you relax and feel connected to the group. Being in a safe, supportive social situation can help you switch from sympathetic to parasympathetic.

Spending time with your children doing a fun project, playing a game, or reading a book together can also help you, and them, to make the switch.

Adults change their tone of voice and facial expressions when speaking with children. We raise our voices up a notch, speak in quiet, soothing tones and put a soft, cheery expression on our faces.

If you go into a kindergarten class, you will often notice the teacher crouching down on the child's level and speaking to young children with a high-pitched, soft tone of voice to the children. This signals to children they are safe and can relax.

We can use this technique with our children if they have experienced trauma to help them feel safe. We can also use it with our loved ones, and we can ask our loved ones to use it with us when they talk to us.

The vagus nerve controls our tone of voice and our facial expressions. The nerve is stimulated differently by how we talk and look. Our child's vagus nerve is getting stimulated by our tone of voice and expressions, as well.

HOW TO CONVINCE OUR VAGUS NERVE WE ARE... 47

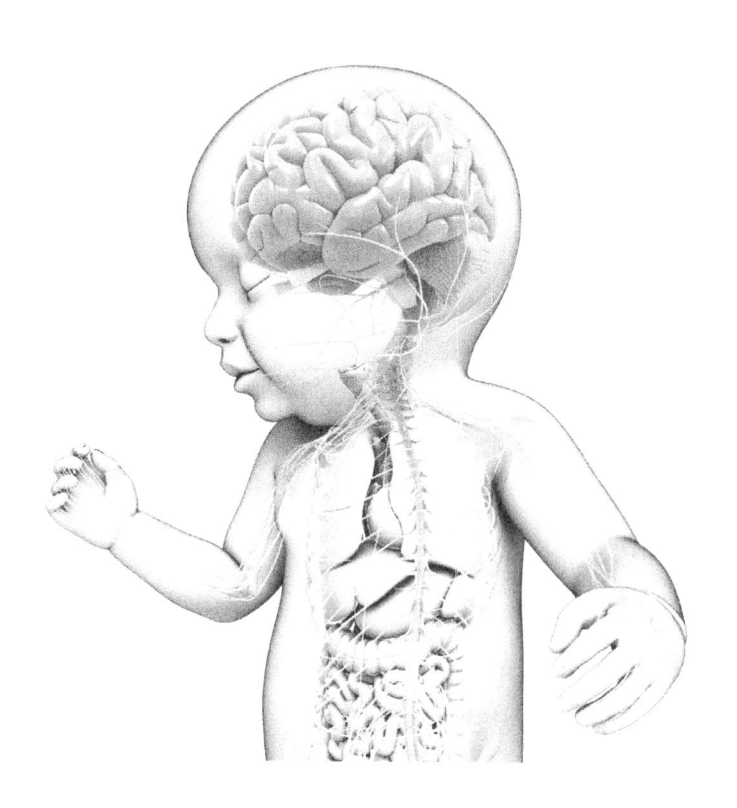

Relaxing our facial expressions and speaking in a soothing tone of voice can help us feel safe. We can send signals of safety to ourselves, and to others, by how we talk.

If you feel stressed or panicked, you might feel your shoulders raise, your tone of voice becomes strained and your brow furrow, this sends a signal through your vagus nerve that you are not safe.

Consciously relaxing your shoulders, softening your tone, and putting a smile on your face can convince your vagus nerve and your brain that you are safe and not in danger.

Take a minute right now to lower your shoulders, take a deep relaxing breath and gently smile.

Did you feel any different when you did this? Note your thoughts on how you felt before, and after.

We will go into more specific things that you can do to get out of fight or flight and into a parasympathetic state and stimulate your vagus nerve in the following chapters.

We will discuss many techniques that will help you stimulate and tone your vagus nerve and help you turn on your parasympathetic nervous system in this book.

I don't expect you to practice all of them daily, but to learn about them and see which ones resonate with you and feel most comfortable for you.

If you enjoy what you are doing, you are more likely to commit to doing the practices daily and it will be more effective for you. What works for me might be stressful for you and vice versa. It will take some trial and error to find what works best for you.

Chapter 6

Breathing for your vagus nerve

Naturally, when you are calm and relaxed, you take deep slow breaths. When you are stressed, scared, or are in pain, your breathing gets shallow and rapid.

Our parasympathetic nervous system controls our breathing when we are relaxed and slows our breathing and our sympathetic when we are in a state of stress and speeds it up.

We use breath control in every meditation, relaxation, or calming activity we practice for our body and mind. We have experienced how controlled breathing can help us calm ourselves, but there is a scientific basis for why it works. When we breathe deeply, we stimulate the vagus nerve and trigger the parasympathetic state.

When we stimulate the vagus nerve with our breathing, it signals our internal organs, our heart, and our brain that we are safe and calm.

By inducing relaxation with our breathing, we stimulate the vagus nerve just as our vagus nerve can cause us to relax.

We can't control most of our autonomic nervous system. We can't make our heart beat slower by thinking about it or intentionally releasing a hormone. But we can control one thing that is usually controlled by our autonomic nervous system.

We can control our breathing.

When we control our breathing, we indirectly control other systems in our body that we have no power over otherwise, such as our heartbeats and the release of the hormone oxytocin, the love hormone.

When we breathe deeply, we tell our brains that we are safe. We signal to our hearts that they can slow their beats per minute because we are not being chased and don't need to prepare to run or climb a tree at any minute.

Our vagus nerve stimulates the release of oxytocin, flooding our system with the hormone. This all signals our brain to relax. We feel calmer and have less anxiety after practicing intentional deep breathing.

Deep breathing activates neurons that detect our blood pressure. When we activate these neurons, they signal to the vagus nerve that our blood pressure is becoming too high. The vagus nerve then secretes the neurotransmitter acetylcholine, which slows the rhythm of the heart.

BREATHING FOR YOUR VAGUS NERVE

Deep breathing also stimulates the vagus nerve by stretching it when it passes through our diaphragm. Deep breathing is one of the easiest and most effective ways to transition to a parasympathetic state. There are many ways to practice therapeutic deep breathing and stimulate our vagus nerve.

Practicing deep breathing regularly, over time, can increase our vagal tone, helping us to switch our system to a predominantly parasympathetic state, turning off our fight-or-flight response.

We can also use deep breathing when we feel ourselves slipping into a fight-or-flight state, are having heart palpitations, or are preparing to do something that makes us nervous such as public speaking.

By controlling our breathing, we can control our response to stressful situations.

Breathing through our nose instead of through the mouth signals our brain that we are safe. When we are stressed, we will breathe through our mouths.

For example, if you are being chased by that proverbial tiger, you would run and breathe through your mouth. We are built to breathe through our nose. Using our mouth for breathing is supposed to be used as a backup or when we are in states of stress. Making a concentrated effort to breathe through our nose is easy and helpful for calming our vagus nerve.

Lamaze breathing is used to help women in labor relax and overcome pain. The organized, controlled breathing of Lamaze, stimulates the vagus nerve. That is one reason why Lamaze breathing is so effective in helping women during labor.

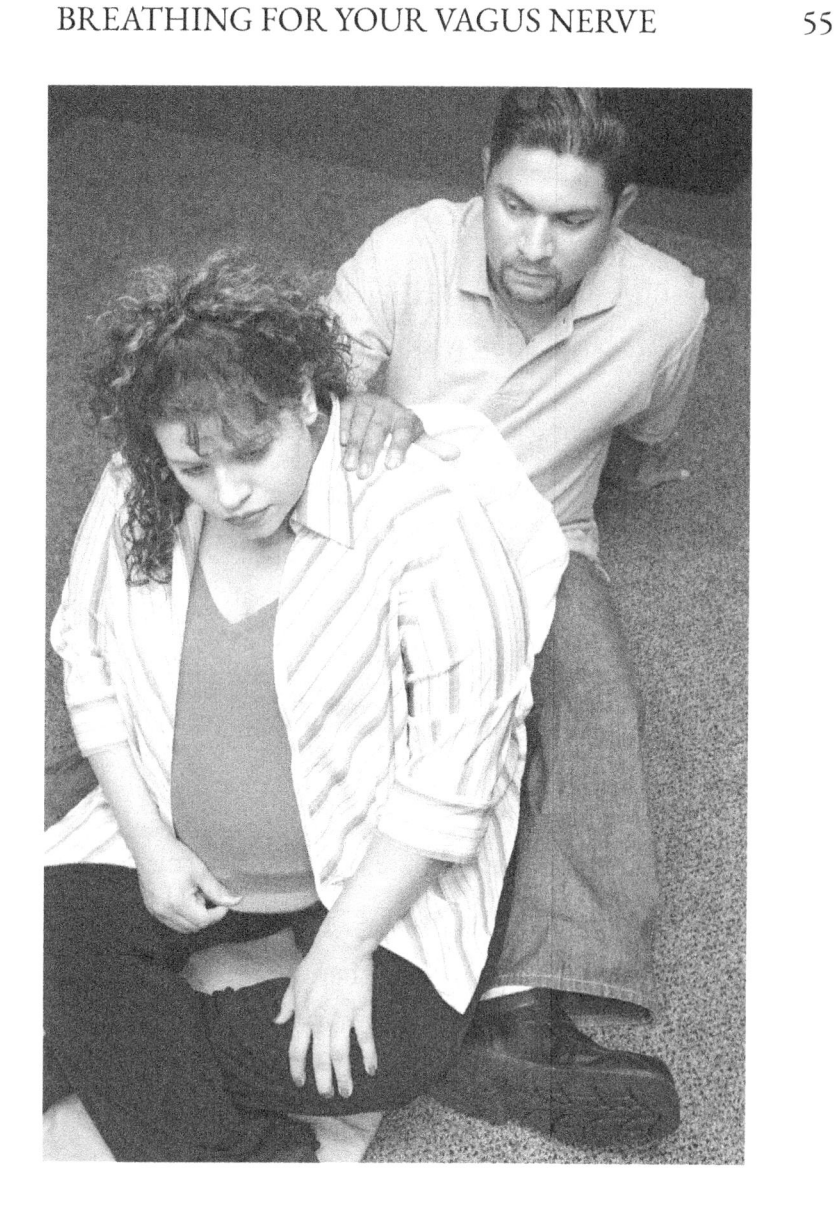

BREATHING FOR YOUR VAGUS NERVE

Knowing how effective it is for women experiencing natural childbirth shows how powerful breathing can be for us in other situations.

Lamaze breathing helps keep women in a parasympathetic state during a very stressful time. Deep breathing helps labor progress.

Imagine women giving birth outdoors thousands of years ago and how vulnerable they would have been. If a wild animal threatened them while they laboring, their fight-or-flight response could slow or even stop their contractions until they were safe.

Relaxing and showing your body that you are safe with controlled deep breathing, allows labor to progress effectively. Using similar breathing techniques can work similarly in other stressful situations.

The benefits of deep breathing are both short-term, getting out of fight-or-flight, and long-term, toning our vagus nerve so it functions better and keeps us in a parasympathetic state. It is also something you can do anytime, anywhere, and for free.

There are many types of deep breathing that you can practice that will help stimulate and tone your vagus nerve.

Breathing in for 4 seconds and out for 6 seconds is a very basic, but effective technique.

Breathing out longer than breathing in bears down on the diaphragm, making it more effective.

Take a moment to try this breathing technique.

Breathe in for a count of:

1, 2, 3, 4............and out for 1, 2, 3, 4, 5. 6.

1, 2, 3, 4............and out for 1, 2, 3, 4, 5. 6.

1, 2, 3, 4............and out for 1, 2, 3, 4, 5. 6.

1, 2, 3, 4............and out for 1, 2, 3, 4, 5. 6.

1, 2, 3, 4............and out for 1, 2, 3, 4, 5. 6.

Nurse friends of mine have told me that medical professionals recommend that their heart patients use the Valsalva maneuver when experiencing heart arrhythmia.

To do the Valsalva maneuver, exhale while closing the throat or bear down when experiencing palpitations. A long exhale works similarly.

If you are an auditory or visual learner and like to use technology, Deepak Chopra and Eddie Stern have created a free app called The Breathing App. You can download it on your phone or tablet.

You can choose a breath pattern that you like. There are 6 options, 2 breaths in, 3 breaths out or 4:4, 4:6, 5:5, 6:6, or 5:7. I recommend choosing one with a longer exhale than inhale, such as 4:6 or 5:7. You choose the amount of time you want to practice, from 1 to 30 minutes.

Finally, pick the screen you want. They have different backgrounds, either a ball that expands or contracts in the rhythm you choose or numbers that count up or down to the setting you have chosen, or if you want to have your eyes closed, there is a screen you can pick with a sound that has a resonant sound that shifts to signal when you should breathe in and when you should exhale.

The app makes it very easy to practice controlled breathing. You don't need to count and can just follow along with the program you have picked for the time you have scheduled.

It is easy if you are just beginning this practice or if you are in public and want to practice with no one knowing what you are doing.

You can also use this app to practice in bed at night. This will help you fall asleep and help you sleep deeper.

It is important to practice forceful inhalation and exhalation with this app and not just gently breathe in and out with the app running. Breathing deeply stimulates the vagus nerve.

BREATHING FOR YOUR VAGUS NERVE

Deep breathing is called Diaphragmatic or Eupnea breathing. It occurs in mammals whenever they are in a state of relaxation or in a parasympathetic state.

When you practice this deep breathing, you send messages to your brain and vagus nerve you are safe and relaxed.

You can do this method of deep breathing without the app on your own, but it takes more concentration and counting.

You can choose the rhythm you want to breathe and then count as you inhale and exhale.

Always exhale longer than you inhale. You want to breathe forcefully enough that your belly goes in as you inhale and out as you exhale.

Take a moment and practice deep belly breathing. Put your hand on your belly and feel it expand as you breathe out.

1, 2, 3, 4............and out for 1, 2, 3, 4, 5. 6.

1, 2, 3, 4............and out for 1, 2, 3, 4, 5. 6.

1, 2, 3, 4............and out for 1, 2, 3, 4, 5. 6.

1, 2, 3, 4............and out for 1, 2, 3, 4, 5. 6.

1, 2, 3, 4............and out for 1, 2, 3, 4, 5. 6.

You can also place your hands on your ribs with your elbows out to your sides and breathe in, feeling your ribs expanding and filling with air, and then breathe out, feeling your ribs contracting as you release your breath.

After you have done this for a while and are comfortable with the technique, you can remove your hands from your ribs and just concentrate on your breaths, breathing with your ribs expanding and contracting.

Wim Hof, also known as The Iceman, has a technique of breathing that works similarly and is very effective for stimulating the vagus nerve.

Wim Hof uses breathing, meditation, and cold tolerance, which we'll discuss in other chapters, to control his autonomic nervous system and his immune system.

Scientists have studied him because his method is so effective. He has also trained others to prove that his methods work for everyone and not just him.

Dutch researcher Matthijs Kox performed a scientific evaluation on a group of 24 healthy volunteers. They were divided into two groups, a control group, and an intervention group.

They trained the intervention group for 10 days in the Wim Hof method, including exposure to cold, meditation, and the practice of controlled breathing.

They did not train the control group.

They then exposed both groups to e. Coli.

The study showed that "In the intervention group, plasma levels of the anti-inflammatory cytokine IL-10 increased more rapidly after endotoxin administration, correlated strongly with preceding epinephrine levels, and were higher. Levels of pro-inflammatory mediators TNF-α, IL-6, and IL-8 were lower in the intervention group and correlated negatively with IL-10 levels. Finally, flu-like symptoms were lower in the intervention group."

Wim Hof and the trained participants produced half the number of inflammatory proteins compared to the average of the test subjects who were not trained by Wim when injected with e. Coli.

The study showed that the trained participants could control their autonomic and immune systems in response to a stressor, the e. Coli toxin in this case, in a way that wasn't known to be possible, prior to the study.

For anyone who struggles with autoimmune disease or inflammation, this is intriguing research.

We can use the same methods to reduce inflammation in our own bodies.

Wim has many videos showing his breathing techniques on YouTube and on his website. He even offers a free mini-class you can take if you are interested in learning it more in-depth.

https://www.wimhofmethod.com/free-mini-class

As a caution, always do any breathing exercises in a safe environment. Do not practice while in the bath, swimming, driving, or in any situation where it might not be safe to practice. I recommend sitting in a chair or couch or laying on the floor or your bed.

Listen to your body and stop if you feel uncomfortable or faint.

If you have serious health issues, please consult a doctor first before practicing.

The basics of Wim's breathing technique are:

1. Sit or lie in a place where you are comfortable and safe.

2. Do 30-40 deep power breaths

Breathe in and out at a steady pace, deeply and forcefully, 30-40 times. Breathe through your mouth. Inhale fully, feeling your belly rise, but don't exhale all the way out.

These are very forceful, powerful breaths that might make you feel you are hyperventilating. You may feel a tingling. This is completely normal and to be expected.

3. Hold your breath

After your power breaths, empty your lungs of air and hold for as long as you can without force. Aim for at least 1 minute. You can increase the time you hold your breath as you improve at the technique, increasing to 2 minutes or even longer. Work on emptying your mind while you empty your lungs.

4. Breathe in for 10 seconds

Take a deep breath in and hold it for 10-15 seconds before exhaling.

5. Repeat steps 1-4 for three more rounds.

According to Wim, this breathing method "activates specific neurons that detect blood pressure."

These neurons signal to the vagus nerve that blood pressure is becoming too high, and the vagus nerve responds by lowering your heart rate.

I find using Wim's breathing technique to be powerful. I experience tingling in my fingers and toes and feel very relaxed but also energized.

Even an hour after doing the breathing practice, I feel an awareness of sensation in my hands that is very interesting and powerful. It feels like I feel the increase in oxygen pumping through my body.

A decrease in carbon dioxide in the blood called hypocapnia causes tingling.

Research has shown that the increase in oxygen in the blood makes the blood more alkaline. When your body is more alkaline, inflammation is reduced and your body can fight off bacteria, viruses, and other pathogens when your system is more alkaline.

The Wim Hof Method is very interesting because the scientific experiments that have been run on him and on people he has trained in his method backed so much of what he does up.

Pranayama breathing or yogic breathing is also very effective for stimulating the vagus nerve and has been studied and proven effective by science. Yogic breathing has been practiced for thousands of years.

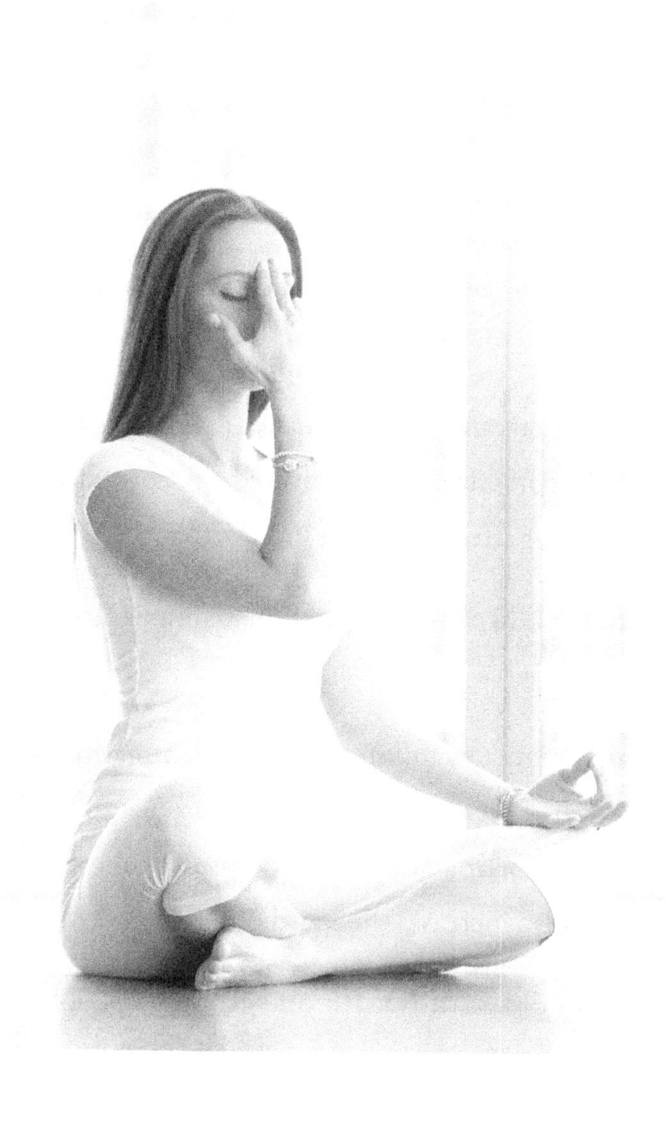

Pranayama means energy breath and is the regulation of breath in yoga. Yogis believe that this breathing circulates energy through your body.

Pranayama is a form of yoga anyone can practice, even if you are chair or bed bound.

Dr. Sundar Balasubramanian, a biochemist, a radiation oncology researcher, and a yoga practitioner, discovered that his saliva had more nerve growth factor after practicing Pranayama.

Nerve growth factor (NGF) causes the growth, maintenance, proliferation, and survival of nerve cells.

NGF is part of what regulates immunity and inflammation. Low NGF, or dysregulation of NGF, contributes to neurological diseases like Alzheimer's and dementia and coronary disease, obesity, and type 2 diabetes. NGF also increases the speed of healing.

Dr. Balasubramanian did a study with one group of people as a control and one group of people practicing the breathing exercises. His study showed that the people who did the yogic Pranayama breathing had more NGF in their saliva, along with an increase in 22 other salivary proteins associated with immune response, stress, and cancer.

I find it so interesting that ancient breathing techniques are being shown to be beneficial by modern science.

One yogic breathing technique is to breathe very deeply, expanding your belly and your chest as you take in the air. As you exhale, hum while breathing out, expelling air from your belly and chest as you hum. You want to breathe out while humming for as long as you can.

Not only does the deep breathing stimulate the vagus nerve, but so does the humming.

Alternate nostril breathing (ANB), or Nadi Shodhana, is another yogic breathing technique. To practice Alternate Nostril Breathing, sit quietly and breathe through each nostril separately.

68　　　　THE VAGUS NERVE COLLECTION

Plug one nostril by pressing against the nostril with your finger and breathing in the opposite nostril. Go back and forth between each nostril, slowly and rhythmically.

Press your left nostril closed, breathe in through the right, then plug the right nostril, unplug the left nostril and exhale through the left, then plug the left nostril, unplug the right nostril and breathe in through the right.

During this practice, have a finger closing at least one nostril at all times. Think of it as breathing air into your head through one nostril and then breathing out that air through the other nostril.

Research has shown that Alternate Nostril Breathing can help lower blood pressure and increase feelings of calm.

A randomized control study by the Patanjali Research Foundation tested 90 participants. 30 participants were a control group, 30 practiced mindful breathing and 30 practiced Alternative Nostril Breathing for 10 minutes.

The ones who practiced ANB showed a significant decrease in their systolic and diastolic blood pressure.

ANB balances the nervous system, evening out differences in sympathetic and parasympathetic tone.

It is an excellent way to turn off your sympathetic nervous system and turn on your parasympathetic nervous system.

Any of these breathing techniques are useful for quickly getting out of fight-or-flight mode. You can practice deep breathing daily to train yourself to stay in a parasympathetic state.

Chapter 7

Cold Exposure to Stimulate Your Vagus Nerve

Cold exposure is increasingly being recognized as an effective way of stimulating the vagus nerve. Cold exposure can help to activate the nervous system and create a calming effect on the body. It stimulates the vagus nerve by sending a signal from the skin receptors to the brain. This activates the parasympathetic nervous system and helps to reduce stress, improve digestion, reduce inflammation and improve overall health.

Cold exposure can be achieved in a few different ways.

The most common way is to take a cold shower or a bath. A cold shower is a simple way to stimulate your vagus nerve daily. Ending your shower with 30 seconds-2 minutes of icy cold water can stimulate your vagus nerve. Cold water therapy also called or intermittent hypothermia or cryotherapy, is becoming more popular as it has been shown to reduce inflammation, improve skin health, and improve cognitive performance. Lowering the temperature of the water (not freezing) for a few minutes will help activate the vagus nerve. Sitting in a cold or icy pool for a few minutes can also help to stimulate the vagus nerve if you have one available. This can help to increase parasympathetic activity and improve digestion.

Breathing in cold air helps to stimulate the vagus nerve. This can be done by going outside when it is cold and taking deep breaths. You can breathe in cold air, either through your nose or mouth. Simply take a deep, slow breath and hold the air in for a few seconds before exhaling.

It feels appropriate that I am writing this chapter while sitting out on my porch on a chilly afternoon enjoying the soothing effect of the cold winter air. After learning of the benefits of cold exposure for the vagus nerve, my husband and I have been making a concerted effort to spend more time outdoors in the cold. It has surprised us how comfortable we can be while sitting out on the porch in 40-degree weather. We might experience some initial shivering, but shivering stimulates the vagus nerve, so that is a win as well. As we relax into the cold, the shivering stops and we feel fantastic and not particularly cold at all.

Cold can trick your body into survival mode, switching you into a sympathetic state. Studies have shown that as you adjust to cold exposure, your sympathetic response declines, and your parasympathetic response increases.

Cold exposure helps us to flip the switch between sympathetic and parasympathetic, working your vagus nerve. Your metabolism increases and you produce more growth hormone, testosterone, endorphins, cortisol, and dopamine. This gives you a rush of energy and makes you feel happy and relaxed. The release of adrenaline gives you a natural high like a runner's high. When you relax, you can endure the cold better and for longer.

Practicing techniques like the breathing techniques we discussed in the previous chapter can help you relax and be able to tolerate the cold for longer.

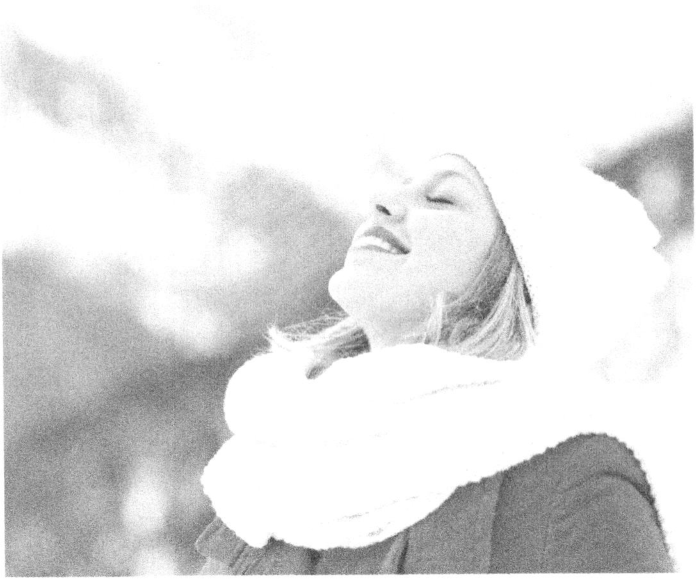

COLD EXPOSURE TO STIMULATE YOUR VAGUS... 75

The cold forces you to switch to the parasympathetic state to tolerate the cold. As your body adjusts to the cold, sympathetic activity declines, and the parasympathetic increases.

When you are exposed to cold, it helps you to tap into the deepest primitive part of your brain. This helps us to move back and forth between the sympathetic and parasympathetic state more easily and stimulates our vagus nerve increasing vagal tone.

Receptors sensitive to cold stimulate the vagus nerve.

We spend the vast majority of our time in our climate-controlled homes, and then take our climate-controlled vehicles to our climate-controlled offices, and spend the weekend shopping in climate-controlled stores.

This is a very recent way to live.

Central heat and air conditioning have only recently become common. We lived for thousands of years exposed to the elements and temperature extremes. Our bodies are made to experience shifts in temperature and to adjust to whatever temperature it is outside over time.

The vagus nerve is involved in triggering our sweat glands to regulate our body temperature, so changes in temperature are a marvelous way to stimulate the vagus nerve.

76 THE VAGUS NERVE COLLECTION

COLD EXPOSURE TO STIMULATE YOUR VAGUS... 77

I end my daily shower with a cold rinse. We have well water. In the colder part of the year, the water is icy as it is coming from hundreds of feet down in the ground, but it is effective to shower with cold water no matter how cold you can get the water in your shower.

When the icy water hits me, it takes my breath away. I inhale sharply, reflexively shiver, and then relax into the chilly water. That stimulates the vagus nerve. Over the course of a minute or two, it doesn't feel as cold as it did initially. You force your body to switch from the sympathetic to the parasympathetic state.

You can work to increase the time you spend in a cold shower as your vagus nerve gets stronger. If you can only tolerate a few seconds, that is fine. You can practice your breathing techniques and work to increase the length of time you can be in the cold water.

If you find a cold shower too hard, you can start by putting your hands or feet in cold water. Work up to putting them in ice water and increasing the time you leave them in the water.

You can also splash your face with cold water. Plunging your face in ice water triggers your dive reflex. This stimulates your vagus nerve both through the cold and from the lack of breathing.

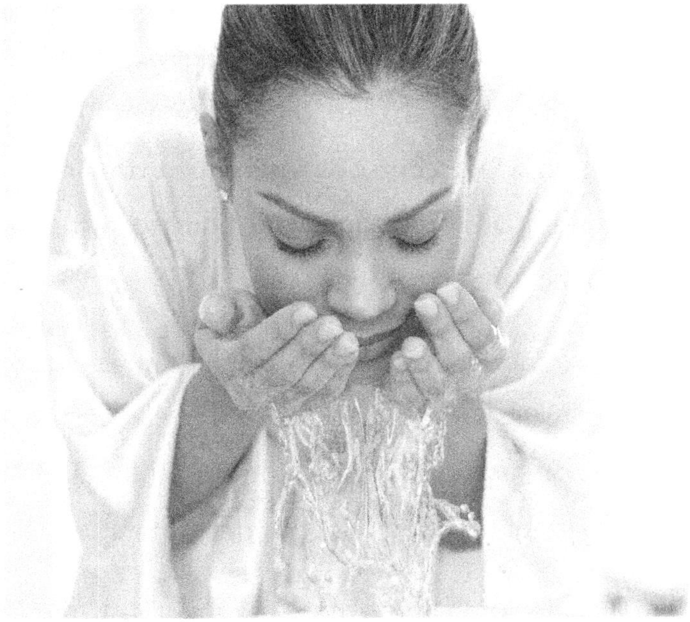

You can also use ice packs or ice to stimulate your vagus nerve. Just be careful to protect your skin so you do not get ice burn.

Going outside in the cold for a few minutes or longer can also stimulate your vagus nerve. If you live in a climate where you have cold weather, you can take advantage of this simple way to stimulate your vagus nerve.

Cold exposure has many benefits for the body and the vagus nerve. It can help to reduce pain, and stress, improve digestion, and reduce inflammation. Cold exposure is one of the easiest ways to stimulate your vagus nerve and is easy to incorporate into your daily routine. It's important to note that cold exposure is not a one-time event. To get the most out of the experience, it is important to practice cold exposure regularly. As you become more comfortable with the sensation, you can increase the length and intensity of the exposure.

Chapter 8

Meditation and prayer

In my research into ways to tone the vagus nerve, one thing that I found very interesting was that many of the rituals that people had been taking part in for thousands of years were also very stimulating to the vagus nerve. For example, church or religious ceremonies can make some people feel peaceful. Many of the parts of the ceremonies including prayers, singing, chanting, or yoga mantras, are also things that are recommended for healing the vagus nerve.

A study found that saying prayers or a mantra increased heart rate variability and lowered diastolic blood pressure. In the study, participants said the rosary, one cycle of the rosary takes approximately 10 seconds or said 6 mantras a minute. This caused participants to breathe at 10-second intervals. Decreasing the frequency of breaths to just 6 breaths a minute increased heart rate variability, which is a sign of healthy vagus function. Meditation or prayer can lower our cortisol and help us relax. A study published in the International

Journal of Cardiology[1] showed that meditation increased heart rate variability, an indicator of vagal tone.

Being a part of a safe community of people is good for the vagus nerve, and when you are part of a church, you have a built-in community that rallies around you.

Music is often a big part of church ceremonies and has been in many religions, ancient and modern across the entire globe. Music is very stimulating to the vagus nerve and can help switch us into a parasympathetic state.

Some religions also practice chanting which stimulates the vagus nerve. Chanting has been used for centuries to help promote relaxation and well-being. Chanting can help to stimulate the vagus nerve and bring balance to the body. During chanting, the vocal muscles contract and relax in a rhythmic pattern, which helps to promote relaxation and a sense of peace.

The practice of chanting is a great way to relax and stimulate the vagus nerve because it is done in a deeply meditative state, with focused attention on the words and sounds being uttered. Chanting can help you reach a state of heightened awareness, allowing you to become more connected to your inner self.

---

1. . https://www.internationaljournalofcardiology.com/article/S0167-5273(07)01323-X/fulltext

MEDITATION AND PRAYER

If you would like to try chanting, here are some ideas to help you get started.

To begin your chanting session, take a few moments to settle into a comfortable position and take a few deep breaths. Close your eyes and focus your attention on your breath. Take a few moments to allow your body to relax and your mind to clear.

As you inhale, feel your lungs expanding, and as you exhale, feel your entire body relaxing. Chant any words, sounds, or phrases that resonate with you. Feel free to make up your own words or use traditional chants. For example, you could chant "Om" or "Ahh" in a low, deep voice.

As you chant, focus your attention on the vibrations that you feel in your body. Place one hand on your chest and the other on your abdomen. Feel the sound reverberating through your chest and abdomen and notice any physical sensations that arise.

Feel your body responding to the vibration and be aware of how you feel in the present moment. If your mind is still racing, take a few more moments to focus on your breathing.

Continue to chant OM, or your preferred sound, for several minutes, allowing the sound to penetrate your entire being.

As you chant, feel the sound activating the vagus nerve and allowing it to release any tension. Feel the effects of your chanting as you relax even further.

Although the Vagus Nerve influences organs outside of the central nervous system or CNS, it is crucial to remember that the Vagus Nerve is rooted in the brainstem and cerebellum. Optimal Vagus Nerve function, or "high vagal tone," is linked to strong social connections, positive emotions, and better physical health. People with low vagal tone index experience depression, heart attacks, loneliness, negative feelings, and stroke.

Brain health and gut health impact one another, and the Vagus Nerve is precisely the connection between the two. The vagal tone index can be considered as the body's "gut feeling" that gets conveyed directly to the brain and produces a feedback loop of more positivity or more negativity.

The autonomic nervous system controls our bodies automatically without us having to engage. Heart rate is a function of the autonomic nervous system. The autonomic nervous system has two divisions, the sympathetic and the parasympathetic. The sympathetic branch is accountable for putting us in fight-or-flight, and the parasympathetic branch is liable for taking us out of fight-or-flight and controlling our bodies when not involved with a fight-or-flight event.

Stress levels are at historic highs and that can cause us to get stuck in fight-or-flight.

Our nervous systems are getting stuck in sympathetic mode, indicating that the changes that take place in our body/mind during fight or flight are not being resolved after the event happens. Consequently, those changes, to varying degrees, stay with us for long periods. This results in chronic stress, which leads to a host of physical, mental, and emotional symptoms.

When the Vagus Nerve gets stimulated through meditation, it affects the parasympathetic branch of the autonomic nervous system to come out of fight-or-flight, decreasing stress.

We know that meditation, especially mindfulness meditation, is useful in lowering stress. Mindfulness meditation is the most studied strategy for meditation, having over 2500 studies published worldwide, with an average of 200 more per month being published.

Mindfulness is the fundamental human ability to be fully present, aware of where we are and what we're doing, and not overly reactive or overwhelmed by what's going on around us.

You can follow mindfulness by sitting down for a formal meditation practice, or by being more deliberate and aware of the things you do each day. Nearly every task we do in a day, for example brushing our teeth, eating lunch, talking with friends, or exercising—can be done more mindfully.

When we are mindful of our activities, we pay more attention to what we are doing. It's the reverse of going through the motions—instead, you are attuned to your senses, noticing your thoughts and emotions. By developing mindfulness into your daily life, you can follow mindfulness even when you're too busy to meditate.

If you're just starting, it can help to choose a short time, such as five or ten minutes. You can build up the time you practice over time.

Many people do a session in the morning and the evening, or one or the other. If you consider your life busy and you have little time, doing something is better than doing nothing. When you get a little place and time, you can do a bit more.

Locate a suitable spot in your home, ideally where there isn't too much disarray and you can find some peace. Leave the lights on or remain in natural light. You can even sit outdoors if you like, but choose a calm place where you won't be interrupted.

This posture exercise can be used as the opening stage of a period of meditation practice or simply as something to do for a minute. Support yourself and find a moment of relaxation before going back into the fray. If you have injuries or other physical problems, you can modify this practice to suit your situation.

How to Sit for Mindfulness Meditation

> 1. Take your place. Whatever you're sitting on—a chair, a meditation cushion, a park bench—find a spot that provides you with a stable, solid seat.
>
> 2. See what your legs are doing. If on a pillow on the floor, cross your legs pleasantly in front of you. If on a chair, it's good if the soles of your feet are touching the floor.
>
> 3. Straighten—but don't harden—your upper body. The

spine has a natural curve. Let it be there. Your head and shoulders rest on top of your vertebrae.

4. Settle your upper arms parallel to your upper body. Then let your hands fall onto the tops of your legs. With your upper arms at your sides, your hands will arrive in the right spot. Too far forward will make you hunch. Too far back will make you stiff. You're attuning the strings of your body—not too tight and not too relaxed.

5. Lower your chin a little and let your gaze fall gently down. You may let your eyelids close. If you feel the necessity, you may lower them entirely, but it's unnecessary to close your eyes when meditating. You can just let what emerges before your eyes be there without focusing on it.

6. Be there for a few moments. Relax. Take your attention to your breath or the feelings in your body.

7. Feel your breath as it goes out and as it goes in. Draw your attention to the physical sensation of breathing: the air passing through your nose or mouth, the rising and falling of your belly, or your chest. Choose your focal point, and with each breath, you can mentally see "breathing in" and "breathing out."

8. Unavoidably, your attention will leave your breath and shift to other places. Don't worry. There's no need to block or

reject thinking. When you get around to noticing your mind wandering—in a few seconds, a minute, five minutes—just return your attention to the breath.

9. Practice pausing before initiating any physical adjustments, such as moving your body or scratching itchiness. With purpose, shift at a moment you want, allowing space between what you experience and what you choose to do.

10. You may find your mind wandering continually—that's normal. Instead of fighting with or engaging with those thoughts as much, practice observing without needing to react. Just sit and pay attention. As hard as it is to maintain, that's all there is.

11. When you're ready, lightly lift your gaze (if your eyes are closed, open them). Take a while and feel any sounds in the environment. Notice how your body feels right now. See your thoughts and emotions. Resting for a moment, decide how you'd like to continue with your day.

It is helpful to try different styles of meditation until you find one that works for you. You can also practice guided meditation. Here is a guided meditation script for your vagus nerve.

1. Start by finding a comfortable position, whether that's sitting in a chair or lying down. Take a few moments to become aware of your breath and let it become deep and slow. Close

your eyes and take a few deep breaths.

2. Now bring your attention to the area at the base of your neck, right between your collarbones. This is the area where the vagus nerve starts its journey through the body.

3. Take a few moments to imagine the energy of the vagus nerve flowing through this area. As you imagine the energy flowing, take a deep breath and allow your body to relax.

4. Now imagine a soft white light radiating from the base of your neck and traveling down the length of the vagus nerve.

5. As the light continues to travel, imagine it connecting to each of the organs and systems connected to the vagus nerve, bringing balance and calm to the body. Continue to focus on the soft white light traveling down the length of the vagus nerve and connecting to all the organs and systems. As you do, take a few moments to become aware of any sensations or changes in the body.

6. Inhale deeply through your nose, and exhale slowly through your mouth. Focus your attention on your breath and let go of any thoughts or worries that may be on your mind.

7. Feel your body relax as you exhale and let your shoulders and neck muscles soften.

8. Now, focus on your breath.

9. As you inhale, concentrate on drawing the breath deep into your body, as if you're filling your chest and belly with air.

10. As you exhale, imagine that your breath is flowing outward and releasing any tension or stress.

11. Now, close your eyes and focus on the space between your eyebrows. Feel the area between your eyebrows relax and soften. Take a few more deep breaths and imagine a soft light radiating from the area between your eyebrows. Allow this light to flow down your face and neck and then relax your chest and abdomen. Continue to breathe deeply and focus on the area between your eyebrows.

12. Bring your awareness to your throat as you focus on your breath. As you inhale, imagine the air entering your throat and circulating throughout your neck. As you exhale, feel the air exiting your throat and releasing any tension or tightness.

13. After a few breaths, bring your attention to your body. Notice any sensations in your body and any areas of tension. After a few moments of awareness, relax any areas of tension by consciously encouraging your body to let go.

14. Visualize a wave of relaxation flowing through your body and feel your body progressively relax.

15. Now, imagine a string connecting your throat to the base of

your spine. Visualize the string emitting a gentle vibration that travels down the string and into your body. Feel the vibration calming your body and mind.

16. Now, with each breath, silently recite the following mantra: "My vagus nerve is functioning optimally. I am relaxed, peaceful, and content."

17. Repeat your mantra on each inhalation and exhalation.

18. Continue to repeat this mantra for the next few minutes. As you repeat the mantra, focus on your breath and the sensation of your throat and neck muscles releasing any tension.

19. Notice how you feel, emotionally and physically.

20. Stay in this state of relaxation for as long as you like, allowing your body and mind to sink deeper into relaxation with each passing moment.

21. When you're ready, slowly open your eyes and take a few more deep breaths. Notice how you feel and how your body has responded to the relaxation.

Integrating meditation, prayer, or mindfulness practices into your daily routine can help you to stay out of a sympathetic state and also give you tools you can use when you find yourself falling into a fight, flight, freeze state.

Chapter 9

EFT, Emotional Freedom Technique or Tapping and the Vagus Nerve

Emotional Freedom Technique is a form of energy psychology that uses a combination of tapping on acupressure points, affirmations, and visualization to help release trapped emotions and energy, allowing you to heal and find relief from physical and emotional issues. By tapping on specific points on the body, individuals can help to reduce their symptoms and experience improved well-being. One way to use EFT for the vagus nerve is to tap on the vagus nerve itself. There are several points on the body that correspond to the vagus nerve.

Tapping works similarly to acupuncture, but without needles. You tap on energy pathways, and meridians to get energy moving in the body. Stuck pain and emotions move, sending a message to the amygdala that everything is ok and calm. The signals tell your body that you are safe.

Along with the physical act of tapping, you follow a verbal script to work on a specific emotion that you want to release. EFT is a combination of ancient Chinese medicine, tapping on the meridians of the body, along with modern psychology, the statements we say while tapping.

One critical aspect of healing our vagus nerve is our ability to feel safe. Tapping is an effective technique to induce a feeling of safety in your body. EFT helps us to cope with our environment effectively. There have been many studies[1] that show that EFT is effective for PTSD, anxiety, stress, pain, and phobias.

Research shows that tapping signals the amygdala, a group of neurons in our brain that processes emotions, memories, and decision making. When you think of something stressful, the amygdala sends signals through your nervous system that there is danger. Through tapping, you focus on the emotion that you are feeling and signal the brain that you are safe.

Tapping can seem strange and uncomfortable, but it has helped many people overcome issues they struggled with previously that standard talk therapy and other modalities of therapy did not help.

---

1. . https://www.eftuniverse.com/research-studies/eft-research

If you have significant trauma, it is best to work with a therapist trained in EFT. They will have the knowledge and training to help you resolve any issues that come up during your EFT therapy. You can find a certified EFT practitioner at this website:

EFT uses a standard sequence of tapping on certain acupressure points near the surface of the skin. Many of these acupressure points coincide with the vagus nerve.

The first step is to identify what to work on.

Can you think of some stress?

Where do you feel it in your body?

What is the emotion that you want to release? Anger, fear, anxiety, panic, frustration, pain, etc.

The more specific you are with identifying the emotion, the more effective the tapping will be. This is an enormous step and can be difficult for some people as we often have a hard time admitting to struggling with pain or emotions. We might believe that it shows weakness to acknowledge something we are struggling with, but this is the first step in healing and releasing that issue.

Identify on a scale of 1-10 how strongly you felt that emotion.

You need not worry about tapping the perfect spots. EFT is very flexible.

Start tapping on the fleshy side of your hand. Some practitioners call this the karate chop point. You can tap on either hand using your fingers from the other hand or use the fleshy side of each hand to tap the other hand. You may have your eyes open or closed, whichever is more comfortable.

While tapping the side of your hand, repeat your setup statement.

Even though I have this emotion or pain (state your specific issue), I deeply and completely accept myself.

Tap the side of your hand while repeating this statement three times.

Now you will go through the acupressure points on your body and tap while repeating the "reminder phrase." Your reminder phrase is the emotion or pain you want to release.

For example, *"This gut pain."*

Tap the top of your head while repeating your reminder phrase.

Tap the edge of your eyebrow near your nose while repeating your reminder phrase.

Tap the bone on the outside of your eye while repeating your reminder phrase.

Tap the bone below your eye while repeating your reminder phrase.

Tap the indentation below your nose while repeating your reminder phrase.

Tap the indentation between your mouth and your chin while repeating your reminder phrase.

Find your collarbone.

Go down an inch and then out an inch.

Tap this spot while repeating your reminder phrase.

Lift your arm and tap on your side about three inches below your armpit. This spot is about where a woman's bra band would be, while repeating your reminder phrase.

Take a deep breath, breathing out longer than you breathe in.

THE VAGUS NERVE COLLECTION

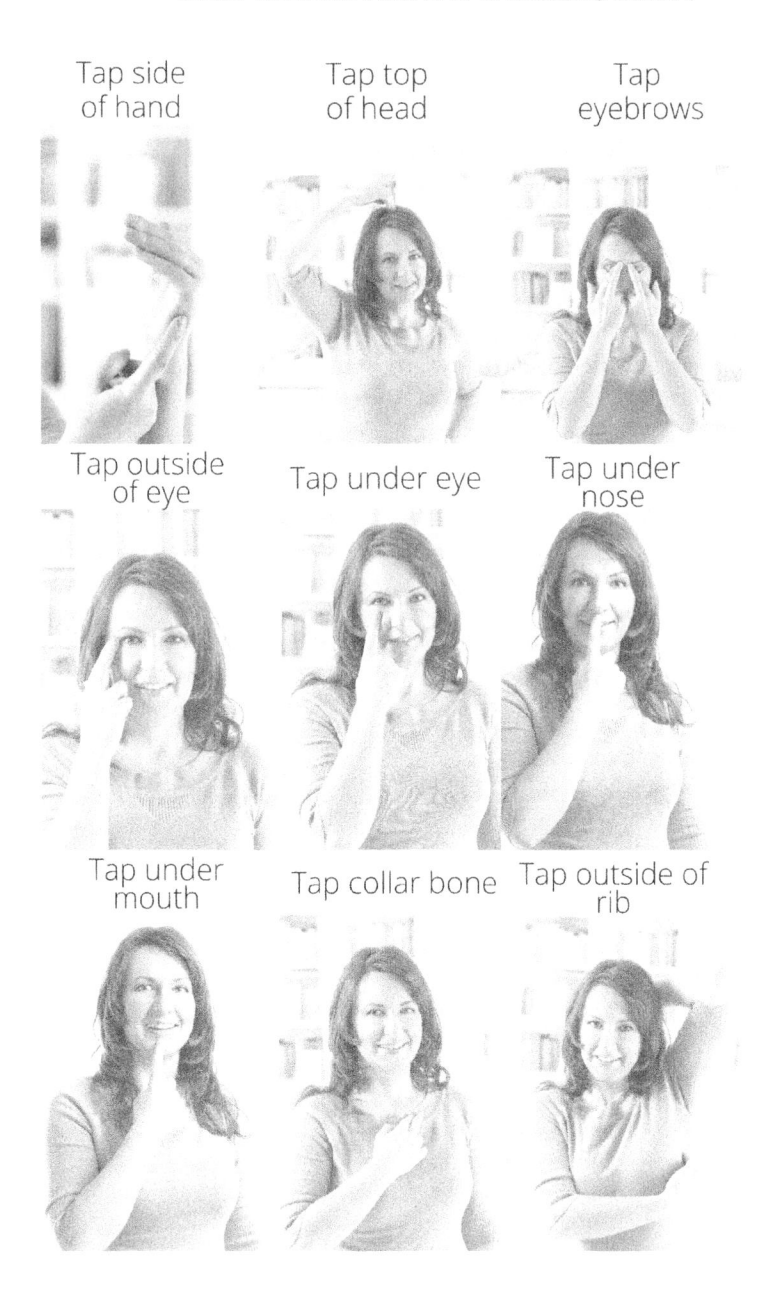

Tap side of hand

Tap top of head

Tap eyebrows

Tap outside of eye

Tap under eye

Tap under nose

Tap under mouth

Tap collar bone

Tap outside of rib

EFT, EMOTIONAL FREEDOM TECHNIQUE OR... 99

Now, evaluate what number on a scale your emotion or pain is after this first round of tapping.

Did your number go down? _____

Did the pain shift? _____

Did something else pop up? _____

It could be work stress, an issue with a family member or friend, or a past trauma. If so, that is a clue of where you need to focus your attention.

You can repeat the steps of tapping listed above with the same statement until you feel the number on the scale go down to where you feel it is gone, you can change your statement to acknowledge the new issue that came up or you can change your statement to reflect that you are ready to release that emotion, pain or trauma.

Here is another EFT script you might find helpful.

Begin by tapping on the karate chop point on either hand and repeat the following affirmation three times: "Even though I have (fill in the blank), I completely and deeply accept myself and my body."

Now tap on the eyebrow point and repeat the following affirmation three times: "I am calming my vagus nerve and activating my relaxation response."

Tap on the side of the eye point and repeat the following affirmation three times: "My body is relaxing and I am calming my vagus nerve."

Tap on the under-the-eye point and repeat the following affirmation three times: "I am releasing any tension and stress from my body and activating my relaxation response."

Tap on the under-the-nose point and repeat the following affirmation three times: "I am allowing my body to relax and my vagus nerve to activate."

Tap on the chin point and repeat the following affirmation three times: "I am allowing my body to relax and my vagus nerve to activate."

Tap on the collarbone point and repeat the following affirmation three times: "I am releasing all tension and stress from my body and activating my relaxation response."

Tap on the underarm point and repeat the following affirmation three times: "I am allowing my body to relax and my vagus nerve to activate."

Tap on the top of the head point and repeat the following affirmation three times: "I am releasing all tension and stress from my body and activating my relaxation response."

Finally, tap on the karate chop point one more time and repeat the following affirmation three times: "I am calming my vagus nerve and activating my relaxation response."

When you feel ready, stop tapping and take a few deep breaths. Allow yourself to relax and enjoy the feeling of calmness and relaxation.

By repeating this EFT tapping script, you can activate the relaxation response and help your body to release any tension and stress.

You can set up a practice to tap once a day, or multiple times a day. Some find it helpful to tap first thing in the morning to start their day off in a calm, relaxed state or you can tap at night before bed to help resolve any issues of the day and improve your sleep. You can also tap while taking a shower, in the car waiting for your child's game to be over, or in the bathroom before a meeting. If you feel tension in your body, take a few minutes to tap.

If the body tension jumps up, then there is more to explore. The increase in tension is a message from your body, telling you that you have more to explore and work on. Your body is giving you a gift through that message, a clue that will help you get to the root cause of what you need to work on.

Chapter 10

Nutrition for Vagal Nerve Health

Good nutrition is essential for optimal health, and the vagus nerve is no exception. If you are looking to maintain or improve vagus nerve health, nutrition should be an important part of your wellness plan.

If our bodies aren't getting enough nutrition in our food, we can enter a sympathetic nervous system response. In a hunter/gatherer society, food scarcity would be a life-threatening situation to be in and would require all of a human's attention to find food for ourselves and our families. Concentrating on eating nutritious food can signal our brains that we are safe and secure.

What we eat becomes the building blocks of the cells in our body. We now have cupboards and refrigerators full of food, but the food is often processed and devoid of the nutrition that our body needs to make healthy cells.

You can eat calories that put pounds on your frame but starve your body of the nutrients it needs to be healthy.

We must nourish our bodies with nutritious foods. We need to heal the myelin sheath on our vagus nerve so the nerve is protected and works properly.

Eating a processed diet with packaged foods and fast foods can starve your body even as you grow heavier.

When you eat whole foods, with lots of colors and nutrients, your body will have the building blocks it needs to heal and feel safe.

Foods to include in your diet:

- Wild-caught fish
- Grass-fed meat
- Organ meats
- Greens
- Sulfur-rich foods such as garlic, onions, cabbage, and mushrooms
- Foods with bright colors like berries, peaches, oranges, and yellow or red peppers.
- Seaweed

NUTRITION FOR VAGAL NERVE HEALTH

These foods can supply your body with the micronutrients it needs to heal your myelin sheath and feed your brain. Healthy fats stimulate the vagus nerve and regulate the activation of our innate immune system, and mast cells in our guts.

Eating an anti-inflammatory diet can help reduce inflammation in the body, which can help keep the vagus nerve functioning properly. Foods like fruits and vegetables, lean proteins, and healthy fats can all help reduce inflammation.

Magnesium helps to maintain the proper balance of nerve cells, as well as their ability to communicate with each other. Without enough magnesium, the nerve may become overstimulated, leading to fatigue, indigestion, and mood swings.

Zinc is also important for healthy vagus nerve functioning. Zinc helps to regulate the neurotransmitters that control the activity of the nerve. Without enough zinc, the nerve may become overstimulated.

Omega-3 fatty acids are essential for proper vagus nerve functioning. Omega-3s help to reduce inflammation in the body, which can help to reduce the stress on the vagus nerve. In addition, omega-3s help to maintain the health of the nerve cells and their ability to communicate with each other.

If you are deficient in potassium, your vagus nerve will not work as it should. Potassium-rich foods include sweet potato, avocado, beets, wild salmon, coconut water, beans, dried apricots, pomegranate, cooked tomatoes, watermelon, spinach, and pumpkin.

The myelin sheath that surrounds and protects our nerves, including the vagus nerve, is critical to the proper functioning of our nervous system. The myelin sheath acts as insulation on our vagus nerve and other nerves in our body. For our myelin sheaths to be strong and healthy, they need Vitamin B1(thiamine) B9(folate) B12 (cobalamin) Omega-3 Fatty Acids and iodine.

Vitamin B1, or thiamine, is especially important for proper vagus nerve functioning. Vitamin B1 helps to regulate the neurotransmitters that control the activity of the vagus nerve.

Vitamin B6 helps to maintain the health of the nerve cells and their ability to communicate with each other. Without enough B6, the nerve may become overstimulated and cause a variety of symptoms. B6 has helped lower my son's tics.

B12 is very important to the making and maintaining of the myelin sheath on nerves. B12 is critical for the synthesis of neurotransmitters like acetylcholine as part of the one-carbon pathway. B12 deficiency can lead to neurological and psychiatric problems. If you are B12 deficient long term, you can experience neuropathy, cognitive problems, and Alzheimer's later in life.

B vitamin-rich food includes grass-fed, organic sustainable animal products including clams, liver, fish, crab, low-fat beef, fortified cereal, fortified tofu, low-fat dairy, cheese, nutritional yeast, and eggs. If you are a vegan or vegetarian, it is especially important to make sure you are getting enough B vitamins.

Probiotics are beneficial bacteria that can promote the health of your digestive system, including the vagus nerve. Examples of probiotics include yogurt, kefir, sauerkraut, kimchi, and kombucha. Eating these foods can help to increase the beneficial bacteria in your digestive system, which can help to keep the vagus nerve healthy.

While you can get these nutrients from supplements, getting them from food is much more effective. Eating a diet rich in colorful organic fruits and vegetables along with grass-fed meats, especially organ meats, can heal our bodies of many diseases and can heal the myelin sheath on all of our nerves, including our vagus nerve.

Even the best nutrition or supplements are not strong enough to overcome a brain and nervous system that is stressed, but they can help to support your nervous system as you heal your vagus nerve.

Multiple Sclerosis is an autoimmune disease that attacks the nerves, including the vagus nerve. MS is a degenerative disease where the immune system attacks the myelin that covers nerve fibers. This causes communication problems between your brain and the rest of your body. Eventually, the disease can cause permanent damage or deterioration of the nerves.

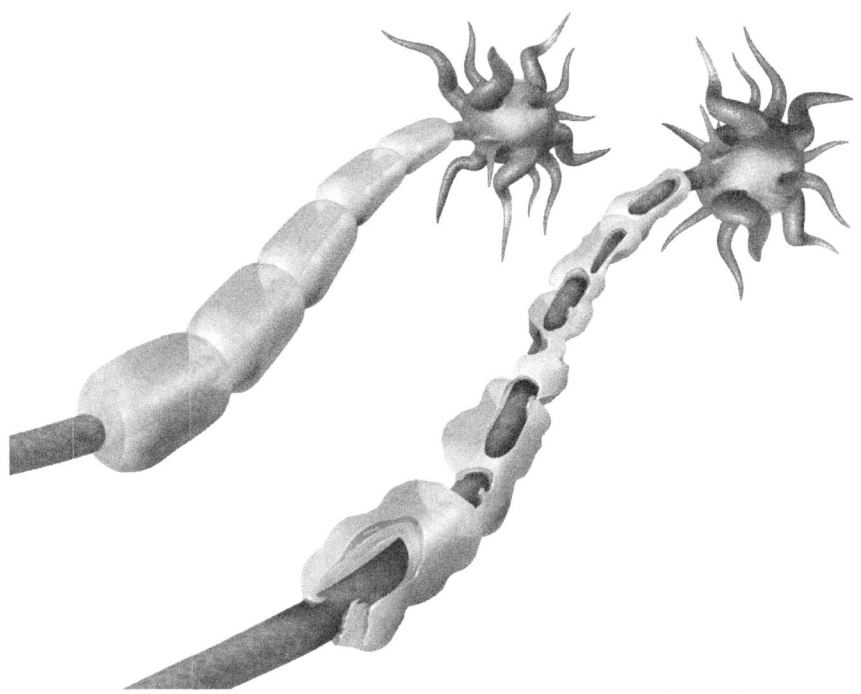

A healthy myelin sheath vs. one damaged by MS

Dr. Terry Wahls has an excellent TEDx talk on her recovery from MS called Minding Your Mitochondria.[1] When I first saw her TEDx talk in 2011, her story of overcoming her illness moved and inspired me. It gave me hope that I could help my family heal.

One thing that most stood out to me was that she was a doctor and was getting the best standard of care treatment available and was getting sicker and sicker until she took her own health into her hands and researched her disease and the causes. She took what she had learned and put together a protocol that changed her life.

You have the ability to do this for yourself and for your family.

Dr. Wahls had been in a zero-gravity wheelchair and was only able to walk a few steps with two canes at her worst. After changing her diet and healing the myelin sheath on her nerves, she now rides miles on her bike.

---

1. . https://www.youtube.com/watch?v=KLjgBLwH3Wc

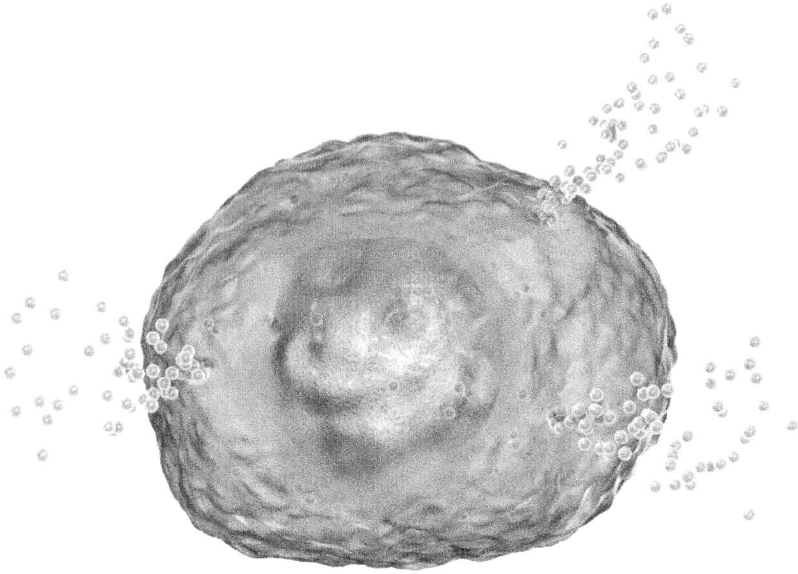

The vagus nerve releases cytokines that regulate mast cells and reduce inflammation. Mast cells can be activated by many types of irritants, viruses, and stressors. When our mast cells are activated, we have increased inflammation. When you have a mast cell reaction, you can have itching, flushing of the skin, swelling, difficulty breathing, hives, low blood pressure, diarrhea, nausea, vomiting, heart palpitations, or hives. When we activate our vagus nerve, we can reduce mast cell activation.

As important as what type of food we eat can be, how we eat is also critical to the health of our vagus nerve.

For many of us, food plays an important role in our lives. Not only does it provide us with the sustenance we need to survive, but it can also be a source of comfort, pleasure, and connection.

But for some, it can be a source of stress and anxiety. Eating can become a source of worry and dread, as we worry about how much we're eating, what we're eating, and how it's affecting our bodies. That's why it's so important to take the time to cultivate calming rituals around eating. By creating a calming ritual around eating, you can reduce anxiety while still enjoying your food.

Rituals around meals like eating together as a family or sitting at the table when you eat, signal our digestive system that food is coming. Our digestive system prepares for the meal by releasing digestive enzymes that help us digest our food.

Here are a few calming rituals that you can incorporate into your mealtimes:

1. Take a few deep breaths before eating. Before you even begin to prepare or eat your meal, take a few moments to take some deep breaths. This will help to slow your heart rate and help reduce your stress levels.

2. Make sure you're eating in a calm environment. Make sure that you're eating in a place where you feel safe, comfortable, and relaxed. Get rid of any distractions and focus solely on the food and your meal.

3. Eat slowly and mindfully. Focus on the texture, taste, and smell of the food. Be present in the moment and enjoy the experience of eating.

4. Don't skip meals. When our bodies are in a state of stress, it's easy to forget to eat or to skip meals without realizing it. Make sure to take the time to nourish your body with regular meals.

5. Listen to your body. Pay attention to your hunger and fullness signals, and stop eating when you're full.

6. Avoid negative self-talk. Don't judge yourself for what you're eating or how much you're eating. Be kind and gentle with yourself.

Mindful eating, and a routine that signals you will eat, can help with digestion issues you may be having.

Chapter 11

How to Stimulate Your Child's Vagus Nerve

Divorce, custody battles, bullying, abuse, prematurity, natural disasters, accidents, medical procedures, parental stress and trauma before conception, during pregnancy, or current stress, can put our child into fight, flight, or freeze mode.

If your child has experienced physical or emotional trauma, they can struggle with issues caused by vagus nerve dysfunction such as anxiety, panic attacks, constipation, diarrhea, digestion issues, sensory issues, sleep problems, oversensitivity to sounds and not healing properly.

Children with neurodevelopmental disorders like autism spectrum, ADD, ADHD, ODD, Sensory Processing Disorder, anxiety, panic attacks, dyspraxia, dyslexia, and learning disabilities can have issues with their vagus nerve and struggle with getting into a parasympathetic state.

When a child is stuck in fight, flight, or freeze mode, they often experience constipation. Our nervous system is programmed to not defecate when we are in freeze mode and for us to be constipated when we are in fight or flight.

The absence of danger is not enough to make our child enter a parasympathetic state. They need to feel safe.

Often, when our child has experienced trauma, we have as well. This can make it very challenging for us as a parent and human beings, to help our child to feel safe when we are traumatized ourself.

Traumatized children often exhibit challenging behavior, making it even harder for us, in our own stressed-out state, to help them feel safe, as we can feel very frustrated with them and have a short fuse. This causes a cycle of their behavior worsening as they feel less safe and us feeling more stressed from their worsening behavior. When we realize that their behavior is a coping mechanism and a reaction to not feeling safe, and that if we help our child to cope, that behavior will dissipate, it can make it easier for us to do the things our child needs us to do to feel safe.

If you think of the old adage of being on an airplane and needing to put your oxygen mask on to be able to help your child put on theirs, working with your child's vagus nerve is similar. We need to regulate ourselves to be able to help our children. It is important that you try to get yourself into a parasympathetic state when you are working with your child and attempting to stimulate their vagus nerve. Children are very sensitive to our moods and stress level. They can feel our anxiety.

Before you work with your child, take a few minutes to practice your breathing or other methods of calming yourself. This will enable you to be more effective in helping your child.

Helping your child to feel safe and helping them get out of fight or flight can help them stimulate their vagus nerve and move into rest, digest, and heal.

A simple way to help your child move into a parasympathetic state is to use the intonation of your voice, speaking to your child with a higher-pitched, melodic, and calm voice. If you gently smile while talking, your child will feel safer no matter what words you are saying. Our voice can give cues of safety to our children.[1] Mothers often will pitch their voices up to a high register and speak in a quiet, soothing way to help calm their children. Using reciprocity, being present, and making eye contact all help your child feel safe, and connected to you and help them.

Singing melodic songs in a higher range is a wonderful way to show your child they are safe. Parents have been singing songs to their children to help them feel safe so they relax and fall asleep through the ages. Disney songs, nursery rhymes, and baby songs are often in

---

1. . https://youtu.be/DNIozAiorZA Dr. Stephan Porges, and Psychotherapists Robbyn Peters Bennett and Amy C. Bryant discuss how we impact our children's nervous system.

this range. Preschool and elementary teachers will often sing calming songs to their students to get them to settle down and be ready to learn. Singling loudly also stimulates the vagus nerve.

Our body posture, getting on the level with the child instead of standing above them can also help. If your child is having a meltdown or you can sense that they are about to lose control in a situation, kneeling down next to them and speaking in a soothing, quiet voice can help them become regulated and help them relax and feel safe.

It is very comforting for children to know what to expect and then have what they expect to happen, happen. Having routine and structure in your home can help them feel safe when the outside world is chaotic. One of the most helpful things you can do for your child is to develop routines for dinner and bedtime that are calming and soothing.

Deep pressure from weighted blankets, weighted stuffed animals, lap pads, or hugs all help to stimulate your child's vagus nerve.

If you feel your child slipping into an anxious state, matching your breath to your child's breath and then extend your breath, exhaling slowly. This can help them calm themselves. Being playful with your child can also help pull them out of that anxious state and make them feel safe.

You can stimulate your child's vagus nerve by working on core strength through crawling, cross-body work, yoga, or dancing with your child.

HOW TO STIMULATE YOUR CHILD'S VAGUS... 117

Massaging your child's back, chest, tummy, and feet with essential oils will stimulate their vagus nerve. Essential oils can help by being absorbed through the skin and also by your child smelling them.

In some cases, you may need to consider other options for your child, such as a specialty TENS unit, to electrically stimulate your child's vagus nerve. Consult your practitioner, chiropractor, or functional neurologist for more information on using electricity or vibration to stimulate your child's vagus nerve.

Meditation can help children become more aware of their emotions and surroundings, and can also help reduce stress and anxiety. Meditation is a wonderful way to help children relax and find peace of mind. It can help them develop a healthy sense of self-awareness and self-regulation, as well as cultivate an attitude of acceptance and understanding. Our goal is to help your child feel calm and safe.

Start by getting your child comfortable in a seated position. Let your child know they can move, wiggle, and adjust their position at any time if they need to. Once they are settled and relaxed, guide them through a visualization. Speak to your child slowly and in a quiet, calm voice.

Here is a basic meditation script that you can use with your child to help them get started.

"Start by taking three deep breaths in and out

Breathe in... and out

As you breathe in, feel the air filling your lungs and heart.

As you breathe out, feel the air leaving your body and bringing with it any negative energy or stress.

Breathe in... and... out

Now, imagine a safe and peaceful place. This place can be anywhere–a beach, a forest, a mountain, or even a room in your own home. Wherever it is, make sure it is comfortable and calming for you.

As you settle into your peaceful place, become aware of your body.

Now, listen to the surrounding sounds. Is there a breeze blowing through the trees? Are there birds singing in the background? Or maybe you hear the sound of the ocean waves crashing.

Now, imagine a ball of warm light. The ball of warm light is coming from all around you. That warm light is love. Love surrounds you. Feel the warmth and comfort of this love.

Take a few more deep breaths and bring your attention to your body. Notice any areas of tension and then let them go. Let any areas that feel tense, relax and go limp.

Now, bring your attention to your breath. Feel the air as it enters and leaves your body. Notice the rhythm of your breath and the way it feels in your lungs and belly.

Notice what thoughts come and go without judging or trying to control them.

Notice how your thoughts come and go like clouds in the sky.

Think about how these thoughts make you feel.

You don't need to try to change anything about your thoughts or feelings, just notice them.

When you are ready, gently move your awareness back to your body and your breath. Take your time and come back to the present slowly. Now, take a few deep breaths and when you are ready, open your eyes and come back to the room."

As you guide your child through this meditation script, remember to be patient and non-judgmental. At the end of the meditation, encourage your child to take a few moments to share their experience with you if they wish. How do they feel? Are there any new insights they have gained? Talking about their feelings and experiences while meditating is a wonderful opportunity to get an insight into your child's worries and concerns. Your attention and support will help them feel safe and loved.

It is also fine if your child doesn't want to share anything that they experienced or thought with you.

Meditation can be an incredibly powerful tool to help children develop a healthy sense of self and gain insight. With practice, your child will reap the many benefits of meditation.

Practicing meditation can help children learn to manage their emotions, reduce stress and anxiety, and improve focus and concentration. Regular practice can also help children cultivate a sense of calm, improve overall well-being, and will help them become more aware of their feelings and to develop their emotional well-being.

Chapter 12

Book 2 Meditations to Soothe the Vagus Neve

Chapter 13

Meditation and Your Vagus Nerve

The vagus nerve is the longest cranial nerve in the body and runs from the brain stem to the heart to the digestive system. It is the gut-brain connection. The vagus nerve is a key component of your emotional regulation, digestion, and heart rate. Known as the "wandering nerve" because it wanders throughout the body, the vagus nerve regulates the heart rate, digestion, and other bodily functions.

Unfortunately, because of a variety of factors, the vagus nerve can become damaged or weakened, leading to a variety of health issues. When it's not functioning properly, it can lead to issues like fatigue, digestive issues, depression, and more.

A part of the autonomic nervous system is the vagus nerve. The autonomic nervous system comprises the sympathetic and the parasympathetic nervous system. The sympathetic nervous system triggers the fight-or-flight response and puts your body into an alert, tense state when it perceives danger. The parasympathetic nervous system brings about a calming, restful state and is often referred to as the "rest and digest" state.

Stress, fear, and other overwhelming emotions can trigger fight, flight, causing the body to go into a state of survival. When in this state, your body is in a heightened state of alertness, fear, and anxiety, limiting your ability to think clearly and act normally. This state of alertness can be beneficial in certain situations, but can also lead to long-term stress and physical illness if experienced too often.

When the vagus nerve is stimulated, it shifts you from a sympathetic state to a parasympathetic state and can help to reduce the body's response to stress, fear, and other overwhelming emotions. Stimulating the vagus nerve has been found to be beneficial in treating depression, anxiety, and other mental health issues, as well as gastrointestinal problems and heart issues.

There are many ways to stimulate the vagus nerve. Cold exposure, triggering the gag reflex, deep breathing exercises, humming, and meditation are some ways to stimulate the vagus nerve.

Meditation is an effective tool for calming the body and mind, resulting in a reduction of physical and mental stress. Meditation activates the parasympathetic nervous system, which helps to counter the autonomic nervous system's fight, flight, or freeze response.

Meditation is a practice that helps to quiet the mind and create a sense of stillness, allowing us to gain insight into our thoughts, feelings, and emotions. When we meditate, we can learn to observe our thoughts without getting caught up in them. This helps to reduce the intensity of our anxiety and develop a greater sense of mental and emotional balance. Meditation is essentially a practice of mindfulness, or the ability to be aware of your thoughts, feelings, and bodily sensations without judgment.

Meditation can help to reduce levels of cortisol, the primary stress hormone, in the body. This can help to bring our bodies back into a more balanced state and restore the vagal tone. When our vagal tone is balanced, we are better able to regulate our emotions and our physiological responses to stress.

Meditation also helps to reduce levels of inflammation in the body, which can help to reduce physical pain and discomfort. Additionally, meditation can help us to better cope with stressful situations and develop a more mindful approach to our lives. This can further help to reduce the stress and anxiety associated with the fight-or-flight response.

Meditation can be done in a variety of ways, such as with guided imagery, deep breathing, or progressive muscle relaxation. Guided imagery is a form of deep relaxation that can help to reduce stress and anxiety, while deep breathing helps to slow the heart rate and reduce blood pressure. Progressive muscle relaxation can help to relax the muscles in the body and reduce tension. All of these types of meditation can help to bring the body back into a more relaxed and balanced state and can help to stimulate the vagus nerve. , but the primary goal is to focus on your breath and become aware of your body and the present moment. Whether you prefer to sit in silence and focus on your breath or use guided meditation like those included in the book to help you relax, the goal is to create a sense of calmness and peace in your body and mind. When you are able to relax and reach a state of stillness, your body can better regulate its systems, including the vagus nerve.

We will explore some of the different types of meditations in the scripts included in this book. I encourage you to experiment with different types of meditation and try different scripts until you find one that works best for you.

Regardless of the type of meditation you choose, it's important to make it a part of your long-term healing plan. Regular meditation practice can help to reduce stress, improve mental clarity, and help you to stay calm and relaxed in the face of danger.

In the next chapter, we'll talk about ways to incorporate meditation into your healing regimen and make it a part of your daily practice.

Chapter 14

How to Implement a Meditation Practice into Your Daily Routine

Meditation is a powerful tool for improving your mental, emotional, and physical well-being. But it's challenging to keep up with a regular meditation practice when life gets busy. When your life is too busy to take time to meditate, that is when you need meditation the most.

Here are some ideas to help you get started on your own personal meditation practice.

1. Set a time: Set aside a specific time of day to meditate, and then stick to it. The best time to meditate is typically in the morning before you start your day or in the evening when you're winding down.

2. Find a peaceful spot: Choose a space that is quiet and comfortable. This could be a corner of your bedroom, a cozy spot in your home, or even a park bench. Make sure to use comfortable clothing as well, since feeling too hot or cold can distract from your meditation practice.

3. Don't overthink it: Meditation doesn't have to be complicated. All you need is your breath and a comfortable seat. If you're feeling overwhelmed, just focus on your breath for a few minutes and clear your mind.

4. Create a routine: Create a meditation routine that works for you and stick to it. Try meditating for five to ten minutes every day and gradually increase the duration as you get more comfortable with the practice.

5. Be mindful: Be nonjudgmental about your practice and the thoughts that come up in your mind. Notice the thoughts, but don't get attached to them. Just let them pass by and go back to focusing on your breath.

6. Get support: If you're having trouble setting up a regular practice, get help from friends or family. Having someone to meditate with can often make it easier to stick with it.

7. Focus on Your Breath: During your meditation, focus your attention on your breath. Notice your inhales and exhales. Don't worry if your mind wanders, just bring your attention back to your breath.

8. Start Small: Don't expect to meditate for hours on end. Start off with brief sessions of five minutes and gradually increase your time as you become more comfortable. Meditating for a longer time isn't necessarily more effective.

9. Give Yourself a Break: Meditation won't always come easily. If you find yourself struggling, give yourself a break and come back to it another day.

Once you have established a regular meditation practice, you'll start to see the benefits it can have on your mental, emotional, and physical health. Give yourself time to adjust to your practice and remember to be patient and compassionate with yourself. Don't be discouraged if it takes some time to get used to the practice. It will become an easy and invaluable part of your daily routine, eventually.

If you're feeling like you're in fight, flight, or freeze mode, the first step is to take a few moments to relax and focus on your breath. Taking the time to focus on your breathing can help to bring your body back into a more relaxed and balanced state, which can help to stimulate the vagus nerve. Once you've taken a few moments to relax, you can then choose to practice some type of meditation.

The following meditation scripts will help you soothe your vagus nerve and get you out of flight, flight, freeze and into a state of rest, digest, heal.

Try the different scripts until you find one that resonates with you. You can use these meditation scripts anytime you are feeling overwhelmed or anxious.

Chapter 15

Meditation to Stimulate the Vagus Nerve

Start by finding a comfortable position, whether that's sitting in a chair or lying down. Take a few moments to become aware of your breath and let it become deep and slow. Close your eyes and take a few deep breaths.

Now bring your attention to the area at the base of your neck, right between your collarbones. This is the area where the vagus nerve starts its journey through the body.

Take a few moments to imagine the energy of the vagus nerve flowing through this area. As you imagine the energy flowing, take a deep breath and allow your body to relax.

Now imagine a soft white light radiating from the base of your neck and traveling down the length of the vagus nerve.

As the light continues to travel, imagine it connecting to each of the organs and systems connected to the vagus nerve, bringing balance and calm to the body. Continue to focus on the soft white light traveling down the length of the vagus nerve and connecting to all the organs and systems. As you do, take a few moments to become aware of any sensations or changes in the body.

Inhale deeply through your nose, and exhale slowly through your mouth. Focus your attention on your breath and let go of any thoughts or worries that may be on your mind.

Feel your body relax as you exhale, and let your shoulders and neck muscles soften.

Now, focus on your breath.

As you inhale, concentrate on drawing the breath deep into your body, as if you're filling your chest and belly with air.

As you exhale, imagine that your breath is flowing outward and releasing any tension or stress.

Now, close your eyes and focus on the space between your eyebrows. Feel the area between your eyebrows relax and soften. Take a few more deep breaths and imagine a soft light radiating from the area between your eyebrows. Allow this light to flow down your face and neck and then relax your chest and abdomen. Continue to breathe deeply and focus on the area between your eyebrows.

MEDITATION TO STIMULATE THE VAGUS NERVE

Bring your awareness to your throat as you focus on your breath. As you inhale, imagine the air entering your throat and circulating throughout your neck. As you exhale, feel the air exiting your throat and releasing any tension or tightness.

After a few breaths, bring your attention to your body. Notice any sensations in your body and any areas of tension. After a few moments of awareness, begin to relax any areas of tension by consciously encouraging your body to let go.

Visualize a wave of relaxation flowing through your body and feel your body progressively relax.

Now, imagine a string connecting your throat to the base of your spine. Visualize the string emitting a gentle vibration that travels down the string and into your body. Feel the vibration calming your body and mind.

Now, with each breath, silently recite the following mantra: "My vagus nerve is functioning optimally. I am relaxed, peaceful, and content."

Repeat your mantra on each inhalation and exhalation.

Continue to repeat this mantra for the next few minutes. As you repeat the mantra, focus on your breath and the sensation of your throat and neck muscles releasing any tension.

Notice how you feel, emotionally and physically.

Stay in this state of relaxation for as long as you like, allowing your body and mind to sink deeper into relaxation with each passing moment.

When you're ready, slowly open your eyes and take a few more deep breaths. Notice how you feel and how your body has responded to the relaxation.

Chapter 16

Meditation to Calm Your Vagus Nerve

This meditation script will guide you through a simple deep breathing exercises that can help to stimulate the vagus nerve and bring about a feeling of calm and relaxation.

Begin by finding a comfortable seated position. Close your eyes and take a few deep breaths, inhaling and exhaling slowly and evenly.

As you breathe, focus on the sensations in your body. Notice how your chest and belly rise and fall with each breath, and take a moment to appreciate the feeling of being alive and in the present moment.

Now, begin to lengthen and deepen your breaths.

As you inhale, notice your breath moving into your body, filling your lungs and expanding your chest.

As you exhale, notice your breath leaving your body, emptying your lungs and letting your chest relax.

With each breath, allow yourself to relax further and further.

As you breathe in, imagine that you are inhaling a sense of peace and calm. As you breathe out, release any tension or stress that you may be holding on to.

As you breathe, visualize the breath travelling down your body and into your abdomen. Feel the breath massaging your internal organs as it moves through your body. Feel your body relaxing and releasing any tension with each breath. Continue to breathe deeply and focus on the sensations in your body. As you exhale, feel the breath traveling up your body and out of your mouth.

Now, place one hand on your belly and the other on your chest. As you take a deep breath in, feel your belly and chest rising. As you exhale, feel your belly and chest falling.

Continue to breathe deeply in and out as you practice this natural abdominal breathing pattern. Take a few moments to observe the rise and fall of your breath. Notice the sensations in your body and how your breath affects them.

If your mind wanders, simply bring your attention back to your breath.

Inhale deeply and slowly, allowing your belly to expand. Hold the breath at the top of your inhalation for a few seconds, then exhale slowly and deeply, allowing your belly to contract.

Repeat this deep breathing exercise several times, allowing the vagus nerve to be stimulated with each breath.

Inhale deeply and slowly, allowing your belly to expand. Hold the breath at the top of your inhalation for a few seconds, then exhale slowly and deeply, allowing your belly to contract.

Inhale deeply and slowly, allowing your belly to expand. Hold the breath at the top of your inhalation for a few seconds, then exhale slowly and deeply, allowing your belly to contract.

This time, as you inhale, count to four in your head, and as you forcefully exhale, count to six, stretching your vagus nerve where it passes through your diaphragm.

Breathe in for one, two, three, four, and out for one, two, three, four, five, six.

Breathe in for one, two, three, four, and out for one, two, three, four, five, six.

Again, breathe in for one, two, three, four, and out for one, two, three, four, five, six.

Now, count to five on the inhale and seven on the exhale.

Breathe in for one, two, three, four, five, and out for one, two, three, four, five, six, seven.

Breathe in for one, two, three, four, five, and out for one, two, three, four, five, six, seven.

Again, breathe in for one, two, three, four, five, and out for one, two, three, four, five, six, seven.

With each breath, imagine the air filling your lungs and circulating through your body, relieving tension and stress.

Notice how your body feels more relaxed and open as you continue to breathe in this way.

Finally, slow down your breathing once more. As you exhale, count to four and let your breath out slowly and evenly.

As you inhale, count to four and imagine the air filling your lungs and relieving any remaining tension in your body.

Continue to breathe in this way, counting to four on the inhale and four on the exhale, until you feel a sense of calm and relaxation in your body.

When you are ready, open your eyes and take a few moments to appreciate the feeling of being alive and in the present moment. Take a few moments to observe how your body feels. Notice any changes in your body, mind, or emotions.

Chapter 17

Meditation to Get Out of Fight or Flight

The fight-or-flight response is an instinctive response to perceived danger or threat, and it's difficult to shut off once something has triggered it. Fortunately, meditation can be an effective way to help you get out of this state of heightened alertness and back into a relaxed, balanced state of mind.

This meditation script is designed to help you get out of fight-or-flight and back into a more peaceful and relaxed state of being.

Before you begin, be sure to find a comfortable, quiet place where you can relax without interruption. Once you are settled, let's begin.

Start by taking a few moments to bring your awareness to your body. Notice how it feels to sit in this space and the sensations of your body as it rests in this moment.

Now, close your eyes and take slow, deep breaths. Notice any feelings or sensations of fear or anxiety. Observe these feelings without judgment, simply recognizing them for what they are.

Take a few moments to focus on your breath, allowing the breath to relax and soothe the body. As you continue to focus on your breath, imagine that the fear or anxiety is slowly melting away.

As you do so, imagine a warm, white light entering through your nose, filling your body and radiating out to the tips of your toes and the top of your head. This light is a reminder of peace and calm.

As you continue to breathe, bring your focus to your heart. Notice how it feels to be here, in this moment, and allow yourself to let go of any worries or stress. Letting go of any fear that is present.

Now, imagine that your heart is a beautiful, glowing sphere of light. Notice how this light radiates out, filling the room and your body with a sense of peace and calm.

Now, imagine a rope connecting your feet to the ground.

This rope is a symbol of your vagus nerve. Feel the strength, stability, and security this connection brings.

Next, imagine the rope connecting your hands with the energy of the rope flowing through your arms and into your heart, bringing a feeling of love and compassion.

Finally, visualize the rope connecting the top of your head with the energy of the rope flowing through your body and out into the universe. Feel the energy of this connection fill your entire being.

You can easily shift out of fight-or-flight mode and into a more relaxed state of being.

Continue to stay here, in this peaceful state, for as long as you need. As you do, imagine that you are tapping into a deep well of inner strength, courage, and resilience.

When you are ready, slowly open your eyes and bring your awareness back to the present moment. Notice how you feel, and if necessary, take a few moments to ground yourself back into the present.

Chapter 18

Meditation to Calm Your Nervous System

Our nervous system is incredibly complex and can be affected by so many things, including trauma and chronic stress. It's important to take time to relax and give your mind and body a break. This meditation script can help you calm your nervous system and bring peace and relaxation to your body, mind, and spirit.

To begin, take a few moments to notice your physical sensations. Feel the pressure of your body on the chair or the floor, the temperature in the surrounding room, and the flow of your breath.

Now bring your attention to your breath. Feel the sensation of inhaling and exhaling as your breath naturally moves in and out.

Now take a few moments to focus on your body, from head to toe. Allow yourself to notice any areas of tension. Acknowledge any tension and then allow yourself to gently let it go.

Once you feel relaxed, focus on your breath.

Notice the rhythm of your breathing and the sensation of air entering and leaving your body. Feel the stillness that comes with a relaxed breath.

Now, take some time to envision a place that brings you peace and calm. It can be real or imagined. It doesn't matter - just choose a place that makes you feel relaxed and at ease. Once you've chosen your place, imagine yourself there.

Feel the sensation of relaxation that comes with being in this place. Spend some time here and really take in the sensations of relaxation and peace.

Now draw your awareness to your heart center and feel the sensation of your heart beating. Allow yourself to be soothed by the rhythm of your heart.

Now, shift your attention to your nervous system. Imagine that your nervous system is a river, with waves of energy rolling through your body. Feel the rhythm of the waves and take a few moments to connect with the energy of your nervous system.

Now, slowly release any tension in your body. Visualize the waves of energy slowly calming and the tension melting away. As the wave of relaxation passes, let go of all mental chatter and just focus on your breath.

Feel your body melting into the ground beneath you. Imagine a feeling of peacefulness radiating through your body.

MEDITATION TO CALM YOUR NERVOUS SYSTEM

Allow yourself to sink deeper into the stillness of this moment. Feel your body becoming more and more relaxed as you surrender to the stillness.

As you continue to relax, feel the sensation of peace and contentment that comes with the calmness of your nervous system. Feel your body and mind coming into harmony.

When you are ready, slowly move your awareness back to your breath. Feel the sensation of inhaling and exhaling, and the peace that comes with each breath.

Take a few moments to sit in this peaceful state.

When you are ready, slowly open your eyes and take a few moments to savor the peace that you have created. Take this feeling of peace and calm with you as you go through your day.

Chapter 19

Meditation to Improve Digestion

For improving digestion, there are many meditation techniques that can be used. One of these techniques is called guided meditation. This type of meditation involves following a script that helps you focus and relax. Here is a meditation script specifically designed to help improve digestion.

Let's take a few moments to settle in and get comfortable in this moment. If you're sitting, make sure your spine is tall and your shoulders are relaxed. You can put your hands on your lap, palms face up or down. If you're lying down, let your body sink into the ground and find a comfortable position.

Breathing in, breathe in the peace and relaxation of the present moment.

Breathing out, release any tension or worries.

Allow your body to become relaxed, your muscles to soften.

Take a deep breath in, and a long breath out, feel the surrounding space, and the stillness of the moment.

Allow your breath to become your ally in this meditation, and focus on your breath as it moves in and out, in and out. Feel the air entering and leaving your body, and notice the sensations of the breath in your chest, belly, and around your lips.

As you continue to breathe, focus on the feeling of relaxation, and scan through your body, noticing any areas of tension. Take a few moments to soften any areas of tension and let go of any thoughts or worries.

Now, focus your attention on your belly. Imagine a warm, relaxing, golden light filling your belly. As you continue to focus on this light, allow yourself to become aware of the sensations of your digestion. Notice the contraction and expansion of your stomach and intestines, the slow and steady movement of food through your digestive system.

Take your time to observe your belly and its functions without judgment or criticism. Now, with each breath, imagine that the golden light is expanding and healing your digestive system. Feel it filling your body with warmth and energy.

Visualize this light slowly healing and restoring any parts of your digestive system that may be feeling out of balance. Let the light fill your entire body with a sense of peace and relaxation.

MEDITATION TO IMPROVE DIGESTION

As you continue to focus on your breath and the light in your body, repeat the following phrase to yourself:

"My digestive system is healthy and strong. I am relaxed and at peace."

With each repetition, allow yourself to feel more and more relaxed. Let the light in your body continue to restore balance and harmony.

"My digestive system is healthy and strong. I am relaxed and at peace."

"My digestive system is healthy and strong. I am relaxed and at peace."

Visualize the digestive process from the moment you take a bite of food through the process of digestion to the elimination of waste from the body.

Imagine your food being broken down and absorbed into the body, and your body being able to get the nutrients it needs from your food.

As you visualize this process, focus on your breath. With each inhalation, imagine the air being filled with relaxation and healing energy. With each exhalation, allow this energy to flow through your body, especially through your digestive system.

Picture the relaxation energy circulating through your digestive system, relieving any tension and discomfort. Visualize your digestive system functioning at its best, with all the parts working together harmoniously.

Continue to focus on your breath and visualize your digestive system functioning optimally.

Allow yourself to be here, in this present moment, and feel the peace and relaxation that comes with this. Take a few more moments to continue to let go, as you allow your body to rest and digest.

When you're ready, slowly open your eyes, taking a few moments to adjust to the space around you. As you move through your day, let the peace and relaxation that you experienced in this meditation stay with you.

Chapter 20

Meditation to Release Anxiety

We all experience moments of anxiety, stress, and fear throughout our lives. Whether it's a fear of failure, fear of rejection, fear of the unknown, or simply feeling overwhelmed, these emotions can be powerful and difficult to manage. That's why having a meditation script to release anxiety can be so helpful. A meditation script can provide a calm, soothing way to quiet the mind and take a break from the stress of the moment. This meditation script for anxiety helps you find peace and relaxation in the present moment. The goal is to practice being in the present moment by focusing on your breath and being mindful of your thoughts and feelings.

To begin, find a comfortable position in a chair or seated on the floor. Close your eyes and take a few deep breaths.

As you inhale and exhale, notice the sensation of the breath in your body. Feel the sensation of your chest and abdomen rising and falling as you breathe in and out.

Now, bring your attention to your thoughts. Notice any anxious or fearful thoughts that arise without judging them or trying to change them.

Now, imagine that your worries, anxieties, and fears are like clouds in the sky. Notice the clouds, but don't get attached to them. Acknowledge them and let them pass.

Imagine your worries floating away.

Imagine your anxieties floating away.

Imagine your fears floating away.

With each breath, imagine these emotions floating away

Now, bring your attention to the area of your body where you are feeling the most tension and anxiety.

Notice the tension and simply observe it without judgment. Breathe into the area, allowing the breath to release the tension. As you continue to breathe, imagine that the tension is melting away with each exhale.

When you are ready, notice the sensation of the breath as it moves in and out of your body.

As you inhale, imagine that the breath is bringing in a sense of calm and peace. As you exhale, imagine that the breath is releasing any anxious or fearful thoughts. Continue to focus on your breath and

MEDITATION TO RELEASE ANXIETY

notice any changes in your body. Notice any lightness or heaviness in your body, any tightness or relaxation in your muscles.

We are now going to use a positive mantra to reaffirm your commitment to relaxation and peace. You can repeat these mantras silently to yourself or aloud as part of your meditation.

"I am relaxed, peaceful, and at ease."

"I am relaxed, peaceful, and at ease."

"I am relaxed, peaceful, and at ease."

"I am strong and capable of managing my anxiety."

"I am strong and capable of managing my anxiety."

"I am strong and capable of managing my anxiety."

"I am safe and I can let go of my worries."

"I am safe and I can let go of my worries."

"I am safe and I can let go of my worries."

Continue to focus on your breath until you find yourself in a state of deep relaxation.

When you are ready, slowly open your eyes.

Take a few moments to bring your attention back to the present moment.

Allow yourself to slowly move your body and gradually come back to the here and now.

Take a few more deep breaths and recognize that you have the power to find peace and relaxation in the present moment.

Chapter 21

Meditation to Release Anger

Anger is a powerful force that can help us protect ourselves and respond to danger, but it can also lead to overreaction and unnecessary negative emotions. By using a meditation script to release anger, you can take a step back and observe your thoughts and feelings, allowing you to gain insight into the source of your anger.

This script is designed to reduce the physical effects of anger and activate the parasympathetic nervous system, which helps promote healing and relaxation. We will focus on releasing anger and connecting with the vagus nerve, also known as the fight, flight, or freeze response. This response handles our body's reaction to stress, fear, and danger. When we get stuck in the fight portion of fight, flight, freeze, it can cause many mental and physical health problems.

To begin, find a comfortable position, either sitting or lying down.

Close your eyes and take slow, deep breaths. As you inhale, imagine a wave of soothing energy moving through your body, starting at the top of your head and moving down through your neck, shoulders, and chest. As you exhale, imagine the stress and tension leaving your body.

Visualize the nerve stretching from the base of your skull all the way down to your diaphragm. Visualize the nerve becoming more active and engaging.

As you focus on this nerve, imagine the energy of anger running through it.

Now, take a few moments to connect with the source of your anger.

Acknowledge the emotion and allow yourself to fully experience it.

Now, bring your attention to the sensations of anger, frustration, or irritation that are present in your body. Notice where they are located and allow yourself to simply observe them.

Acknowledge and accept any anger you feel without judgment.

Now, focus on the source of your anger.

Remember the situation or person who made you angry. Notice the thoughts, emotions, and physical sensations that arise in your body.

Allow yourself to feel these emotions without judgment or resistance.

MEDITATION TO RELEASE ANGER

Take a few moments to imagine how you would like to feel instead. As you do, imagine that your vagus nerve is releasing the energy of anger, allowing it to dissipate and move out of your body.

On each out-breath, soften your body around the sensation of anger. As you do this, imagine that the sensation is slowly releasing from your body. Continue to breathe deeply and with each out-breath, allow the sensation to slowly melt away.

Now, focus your attention on the space that is left behind. Allow yourself to fill this space with compassion, understanding, and acceptance. Continue to breathe deeply and focus your attention on the space that is left behind. Now, give yourself permission to release any remaining anger, frustration, or irritation. With each out-breath, allow yourself to let go of any negative emotions that remain.

Focus your attention on any physical sensations, such as a tingling in your limbs or a warmth throughout your body. With each breath, imagine the relaxation spreading throughout your body and the anger dissipating.

Imagine a ball of light in your hands. Visualize the light growing brighter and brighter until it is so bright that it is almost blinding. Imagine the bright white light filling your body. This is the light of peace and calm that will help to dissipate the anger and wash away all the negative energy and emotions.

Visualize the light slowly spreading throughout your body, starting from your head and traveling down to your toes. As it passes through your body, the anger dissipates and you feel calmer and more at peace. Continue to visualize the light and allow yourself to feel the peace and quiet that it brings.

Continue to breathe deeply and allow the relaxation to fill your body.

Focus on the feeling of peace and calm that is now present in your body. Visualize yourself in a calm and peaceful place.

Take a few moments to relax and soak up the feeling of peace and contentment. When you are ready, open your eyes and give yourself a few moments to come back to the present.

Chapter 22

Meditation to Release Fear

We all experience fear in our lives, and it can often be overwhelming and difficult to manage. Fear can come in many forms, like fear of failure, fear of the future, fear of the unknown, or fear of rejection. By learning how to tap into mindfulness and meditation, we can become better equipped to manage and even lessen our fear.

This meditation script is designed to help you to release your fear and find more peace and calm in your life.

Begin by finding a comfortable position, either seated or lying down.

Close your eyes and focus your attention on your breath. As you inhale, feel your chest, belly and rib cage expand. As you exhale, feel the tension releasing from your body.

Allow your body to relax and let go of any tension or stress.

Now, focus on the fear that is present within you. Notice how it feels in your body. Identify the parts of your body that feel uncomfortable, tense, or tight.

As you notice the fear, imagine it gradually flowing out of your body and dissipating into the atmosphere.

Now, bring your attention to the area of your body where you felt fear the most. It could be your stomach or chest, or any other area of your body. Focus on this area and notice how your body feels at this moment. Is it tight? Is it relaxed?

Allow yourself to experience whatever sensations arise without judgment.

Now, imagine that fear is a deep pool of energy located in this area of your body. Take a few moments to visualize this energy and feel its intensity. Now, release this fear from your body.

Allow yourself to surrender to the process. You may feel a physical or emotional release, or you may simply feel a sensation of peace.

As you release the fear, notice any beliefs that may be associated with it. Allow yourself to let go of any stories, judgments, or patterns that arise.

Now, focus on what you want to feel instead of fear. Visualize a feeling of peace and relaxation, filling your body with calm and soothing energy.

MEDITATION TO RELEASE FEAR

Imagine yourself in a safe and protected space, feeling safe and secure. This could be a place in nature, a beach or a mountain, or a room of your own. Imagine yourself in this peaceful place and feel the warmth and safety that it brings.

Now, bring your awareness to the area in your body where the fear is located. Notice how it feels and the sensations that come with it. Let the fear be there, but don't judge it or push it away. Notice how it affects your body.

Now, bring your attention to your breath.

As you inhale, imagine a warm, golden light coming into your body, melting away the fear and calming your mind. As you exhale, imagine releasing the fear and all the accompanying thoughts.

Continue to breathe and focus on the light, allowing it to fill your body and bring peace and calm.

Now, take a few moments to sit with this feeling of peace and calm, noticing how it affects your body and mind.

When you're ready, slowly open your eyes.

Take a few moments to look around and consider how you're feeling. Take this feeling of peace and calm with you throughout your day and use it to help you move through moments of fear.

Chapter 23

Meditation to Release Resentment

Resentment can be a powerful emotion. It can lead to feelings of anger and helplessness and can prevent us from being our best selves. Do you feel like you're carrying around the weight of resentment due to something that has happened in the past? Maybe you can't seem to let go of the hurt and anger you feel toward someone else and it's keeping you from feeling truly free. Resentment can also be a hard emotion to let go of, but with practice and intention, we can move away from that negative place.

To begin, take a few moments to sit in stillness and observe your breath. Feel each inhale and exhale, and allow yourself to notice your body.

Now, bring your attention to the area of your body where you feel resentment. Notice how it feels in your body, and what emotions and thoughts come up when you think about it. Notice the sensations you feel in your body -- tension, tightness, heat, or cold. Take a few moments to focus on these sensations as you explore them. Don't be afraid of what you feel--just observe it and acknowledge it.

Now, imagine that the resentment you are feeling is a heavy weight that is pressing down on your body. Notice how the weight feels and the sensations it creates.

Picture a balloon. The balloon is filled with all the resentment you're carrying, and it's slowly growing bigger and bigger as you fill it with more and more resentment.

Now imagine a large white light surrounding the balloon.

With each breath, the light grows brighter and brighter, until it completely envelopes the balloon. Visualize the light slowly melting away the resentment. With each breath, the light loosens the grip of resentment, and it drifts away from you.

Finally, imagine the balloon rising into the sky and disappearing.

Now, allow yourself to let go of the resentment and anger. Imagine that the weight is slowly lifting away from your body, leaving you feeling lighter and freer.

As the weight lifts away from you, notice how the feelings of resentment and anger change. Notice how the intensity of the feelings begins to lessen and eventually fades away.

Now, imagine you are holding a soft, white light in your hands. Feel the warmth of the light, and imagine it radiating out and surround-

MEDITATION TO RELEASE RESENTMENT

ing your body. Allow the light to fill your body with a feeling of warmth and compassion.

As the feelings fade away, take a few moments to just sit with the feelings of peace and freedom that come up in their place. Allow yourself to enjoy the feeling of liberation and freedom.

Take a few moments to observe the sensation of your body without the resentment. Feel the warmth, peace, and openness that comes with it.

Notice how the weight of resentment and anger has lifted away and how you feel a sense of inner freedom and peace. Let this feeling of peace and freedom be your reminder that you are strong enough to let go of the past and move forward with a lighter heart.

Finally, when you're ready, slowly open your eyes. Take a few moments to appreciate the peaceful feeling that comes with releasing resentment.

Chapter 24

Meditation for Deep Sleep

Meditation is a great way to relax your body and mind and get a good night's sleep. This meditation script for deep, restful sleep will help you to relax and drift off into a restful and restorative sleep.

Before we begin, lie down on your bed and close your eyes.

Focus on your breathing and allow yourself to relax in the moment. Feel your body become heavy and sink into the bed beneath you.

Feel the air entering your nose and filling your lungs. When you exhale, feel your chest and abdomen relax, and your body sink further into the ground. Take one more deep breath and let it out as a sigh.

Allow yourself to relax even deeper into the bed.

As you meditate, pay attention to any thoughts that come into your mind. Acknowledge these feelings without judgment and then return your focus to the sensation of your breath. Feel the air entering your nose and filling your lungs. As you exhale, feel your chest and abdomen relax, and your body sink further into the ground.

As you continue to breathe, feel your muscles begin to soften and your mind and body drift away into a peaceful state.

Now, begin to focus on the sound of your breath. Hear each inhale and each exhale. Listen to the rhythm of your breath and allow yourself to become deeply relaxed.

Begin to imagine a warm, comforting light surrounding you. Feel a sense of safety and relaxation as the light envelops your body.

Notice the rise and fall of your abdomen as you breathe in and out. Observe the rhythm of your breath without trying to change it. Allow your breath to become slow and steady.

Begin to count each inhalation and exhalation backward from 10.

As you count, allow your body to relax even more.

9

8

7

6

5

4

3

2

1

When you reach zero, begin again.

Continue this practice until you feel your body and mind relax completely.

Now, take a few more deep breaths and imagine that you're falling asleep.

Feel yourself drifting off into a deep and restful sleep. When you feel you've reached a deep state of relaxation, you will allow yourself to drift off to sleep knowing that you'll wake up feeling refreshed and rejuvenated.

Place your hand on your chest and bring your attention to your heartbeat. Feel the rhythm of your heart beating. Let this slow, steady rhythm carry you into a deep and restful sleep.

Chapter 25

Meditation for an Inner Sense of Connection and Belonging

In this session, we will explore how to cultivate an inner sense of connection and belonging within yourself, so that it can radiate outward and be shared with the wider world.

First, find a comfortable position and close your eyes. Take a few moments to settle into your body and get comfortable. Allow your body to relax and sink into the ground, feeling the support beneath you.

Take a few moments to simply observe the breath and notice what thoughts come up.

Take a few deep breaths in and out. Feel your breath travel through your body, allowing yourself to feel grounded, safe, and secure.

Now, imagine a place where you feel a deep sense of belonging. This can be a physical location, such as a childhood home, or it can be a mental space, like a happy memory.

Wherever it is, take some time to explore this place in detail. Notice the sights, sounds, smells, any emotions that come up, and any sensations in your body as a result of these.

Notice what you are feeling in your body. Allow yourself to feel whatever emotions come up. Embrace them and bring them into your heart. Remind yourself that you are worthy of feeling a sense of belonging and connection.

Now, bring your awareness to the energy of your heart. Feel the warmth of your heart and be open to the possibility of feeling a sense of belonging.

Imagine yourself surrounded by a circle of beautiful, supportive, and loving people. Feel the warmth of their love and acceptance for you. Notice how their presence brings you a sense of security and belonging.

Allow yourself to relax into the feeling of being in this circle. Notice the warmth and compassion radiating from these people. Feel the sense of connection and belonging that they offer. Breathe deeply and receive their love. Feel the peace and security that comes with knowing you have a place to belong.

MEDITATION FOR AN INNER SENSE OF CONNEC... 173

Now, imagine the energy of the group moving outward and surrounding you in a field of unconditional love. Feel the warmth of this energy wrap around you and fill you with a feeling of belonging.

Allow yourself to savor this feeling. Allow yourself to receive the love and acceptance of the group. Feel the feeling of support, security, and belonging become stronger inside of you. Feel the energy of belonging that you have cultivated and allow it to expand outward. Notice how this feeling radiates outward and connects you to something larger than yourself.

Sense how it can help you feel part of the human experience.

Stay here with this feeling for a few moments, allowing yourself to be embraced by the energy of love and acceptance. Give yourself permission to take this feeling of belonging with you wherever you go. Take a few more deep breaths in and out. Invite this feeling of belonging to stay with you throughout your day.

Now, slowly return your attention to the breath and gently open your eyes. Take a few moments to sit with this feeling of connection and belonging and let it permeate your being. When you're ready, you can move on with your day, feeling more connected and at ease in your body and soul.

Chapter 26

Meditation to Reduce Inflammation

Meditation is a powerful tool for reducing inflammation, a state that can lead to various health problems. Inflammation is a natural and beneficial response which helps protect us from injury and infection, yet when it is out of balance, it can cause chronic pain, exhaustion, and other ailments. Conditions associated with inflammation include pain, rigidity, and other symptoms linked to chronic diseases, such as arthritis, lupus, and fibromyalgia. Stress, poor diet, and other lifestyle choices can also be causes of inflammation.

Fortunately, meditation can reduce inflammation and its associated symptoms. Through regular meditation, you give your body the opportunity to heal and restore itself.

Here is a simple meditation script:

Find a comfortable spot to sit or recline. Close your eyes and take several deep breaths. Bring your attention to your breathing.

Notice the sensations of your breath as it enters and exits your body.

Now bring your attention to your body and scan it for areas of tension or discomfort. Notice any areas of inflammation that you can feel. Notice how the inflammation feels, and how it affects your body.

Take a few moments to visualize the inflammation as a bright, vibrant color. Picture it growing more intense and bright with each breath.

Now, imagine the color shifting and changing, becoming softer and more muted. Imagine the soothing golden light entering your body in these areas. This light is the healing power of the Universe and it is here to help reduce the inflammation.

As this light enters your body, direct it to the areas of inflammation and imagine it healing and soothing the inflammation. Feel the area becoming soft and relaxed as the light and healing energy gently melts away the inflammation.

Continue to focus on the light entering your body and healing the inflammation.

Feel the pain and discomfort fading away as the light works its magic. Continue to breathe deeply and focus on the soothing, healing light until you feel the inflammation has been reduced.

MEDITATION TO REDUCE INFLAMMATION

Bring your attention to the center of your chest. Visualize the warm, calming light filling your chest. Allow the light to spread throughout your body, bathing your cells in its warmth.

Notice the warmth and allow it to penetrate any areas of inflammation.

Take a few deep breaths and notice the way each breath feels in your body. As you continue to breathe, notice how your body relaxes. Feel the inflammation melting away, as if it were melting away under the warmth of the sun. Continue to focus on your breath and the relaxing feeling in your body as the inflammation fades away.

Take a few moments to focus on the sensations of warmth and relaxation.

Picture the inflammation reducing and your body healing itself.

When you're ready, open your eyes and take a few more deep breaths. Notice how your body feels and how much of the inflammation has been reduced. Take a moment to thank yourself for taking the time to reduce the inflammation in your body. You deserve to feel good and to enjoy your life without the pain and discomfort of inflammation.

Chapter 27

Meditation for Healing and Peace

With this meditation script, you will be taken on an inner journey to a place of healing and peace. Take your time and be gentle with yourself as you go through this meditation.

Begin by finding a comfortable, quiet space where you can be alone and uninterrupted.

Close your eyes and take a few deep breaths, allowing your body and mind to relax.

Focus your attention on your breath. Feel the air moving in and out of your lungs. Notice the sensation of the air passing through your nostrils and the sensation of your chest rising and falling with each breath.

As you continue to breathe, become aware of the sensations in your body. Notice any areas of discomfort or tension. Take a few moments to consciously relax any areas of tension. As you do this, imagine a healing energy emanating from your breath and entering these areas of tension.

Visualize a beautiful, peaceful place. It can be a beach, a forest, a garden, or any other place that brings you a sense of peace and tranquility. As you continue to breathe deeply, imagine yourself in this place. Notice the colors, sounds, smells, and feelings that this place brings to you.

Allow yourself to sink into the peace and relaxation of this place. Feel the soothing energies it brings to you. Imagine that these energies are healing and nourishing you, restoring balance and harmony in your body and mind.

Spend some time in this place, allowing the energies to flow through you, restoring balance and harmony.

Now, bring your focus to any emotional pain or distress you may be experiencing.

Take a few moments to sit with this feeling and acknowledge it. Then, imagine this feeling being washed away with each breath, replaced with a feeling of peace and well-being.

As you continue to breathe, repeat these affirmations with me, either silently or out loud.

"I am healing with every breath I take,"

"I am strong and capable of healing,"

MEDITATION FOR HEALING AND PEACE

"I am surrounded by love and healing energy."

Now, take a few moments to visualize a bright healing light.

Imagine the light is entering your body through the crown of your head and flowing down through the rest of your body. Allow the light to fill your body with a feeling of warmth and healing. Feel it seeping into every cell, bringing a sense of wholeness and balance.

As the light continues to flow, imagine that it is washing away any negative thoughts, emotions, or memories that have been holding you back. Visualize them being carried away by the light, dissolving and releasing their hold on you.

Allow yourself to feel the sensation of being healed. Feel the nourishment of the light as it flows through your body, bringing peace and wellbeing.

Stay in this state of awareness for as long as you need, and then slowly bring your attention back to the present moment. Take a few deep breaths and gently open your eyes, feeling refreshed and energized.

Take a few moments to feel the effects of the meditation, and to journal any insights or feelings that arise.

Chapter 28

Meditation for Autoimmune Disease

Auto-immune disorders occur when the body's own immune system attacks the body's own cells and tissues, leading to inflammation and pain. One of the more recent medical applications of meditation has been in reversing auto-immune disorders, such as lupus, rheumatoid arthritis, Crohn's, and multiple sclerosis.

By meditating regularly, people can reduce stress and improve the body's immune system, which can in turn help to reverse the symptoms of auto-immune diseases.

Take a few moments to become comfortable and relaxed in your meditation space.

Inhale deeply and slowly, allowing your body to expand and relax on the exhale. Bring your attention to your breath, noticing the sensations of the breath entering and leaving the body.

Take time to become aware of your body and the sensations taking place within.

Allow the breath to move through the body, gently releasing any tension or blockages.

As you continue to breathe deeply, focus your attention on your body, noticing any areas of tension. As you pay attention to any areas of tension, imagine a warm, soothing light slowly filling these areas, helping them to relax and release.

Now, focus your attention on your abdominal area, the area around your belly button. Imagine a warm, peaceful energy radiating from this area. Feel the warmth, and allow it to spread outwards to the other areas of your body. As the warmth reaches each area, imagine it filling those areas with healing energy, helping to reduce inflammation.

Continue to focus your attention on the warmth of your abdominal area and allow it to spread further out across your body. Feel the warmth as it spreads, helping to reduce inflammation, and aiding in your body's natural healing process.

Now, visualize a beautiful white light surrounding your body, a light that is filled with love, healing energy, and protection. As this white light envelops your body, feel it healing and protecting you from any further inflammation or damage.

The healing light is permeating your cells and tissues with warmth and healing. Feel the healing light entering every cell in your body, restoring life and balance to the auto-immune system. Imagine the healing light cleansing any toxins, and slowly healing the immune system.

Imagine this white light healing and repairing any damaged cells or tissues in your body. Feel the energy of the white light entering your body and bringing peace and relaxation.

Visualize this white light pushing out any negative thoughts or feelings that you may be having.

Allow this healing light to remain with you as you continue to meditate.

Finally, spend a few moments reflecting on how this meditation experience has made you feel. Notice any changes that may have occurred within you, such as feeling more relaxed or having more energy. Allow yourself to remain in this peaceful state of mind for as long as you need to. When you're ready, slowly bring your awareness back to the room and to your breath. Thank yourself for taking the time to meditate and for the healing taking place.

Chapter 29

Meditation for PTSD

PTSD can often feel like an overwhelming and unmanageable experience. Symptoms of PTSD may include difficulty sleeping, intrusive memories, hyper-arousal, and avoidance. Meditation can be a powerful tool for managing the symptoms of PTSD.

Begin by finding a comfortable position. You can be sitting or lying down.

Close your eyes and take a few deep breaths. Feel the air entering your lungs and exiting your body.

Now, focus on your body. Scan your body from head to toe. Notice any areas of tension or tightness. Take a few deep breaths and let the tension go.

Now, bring your awareness to your heart. Imagine a warm, white light radiating from your heart. Allow this warm light to fill your body with a sense of safety and calm.

Next, bring your awareness to your breath. Notice the rhythm of your breath and focus on the sensation of air entering and exiting your body. Inhale peace and exhale any tension or stress. Allow yourself to relax into the rhythm of your breath.

Focus on each breath and allow yourself to relax into the moment.

Now bring your attention to the surrounding sounds. Listen to any noises that come and go and just observe them without judgment.

As you continue to focus on your breath, slowly notice any physical sensations you may be feeling. Notice any areas of tightness or tension and take a few moments to relax and soften those areas.

Now, take your awareness inward and focus on your emotions. Notice any feelings that arise and take a few moments to observe them without judgment. Notice the sensations they bring and allow them to be without trying to push them away.

Now, imagine yourself in a peaceful place of your choosing. This can be a beach, a mountain, a forest, or anyplace else that brings you comfort and peace. Take some time to explore this place, noticing the colors, smells, and sounds that it offers. Feel the warmth and safety of this place and allow yourself to relax into the peace and tranquility it offers.

Stay in this place for as long as you'd like and then, when you're ready, slowly come back to the present moment. Notice the sights, sounds, and smells around you. Let go of any thoughts or worries that come up.

Notice the peace and stillness that surrounds you. When you are ready, slowly move your body and open your eyes. Notice any changes you may have experienced during the meditation. Take this peace and calm with you into your day.

Chapter 30

Meditation for IBS

Meditation for IBSMeditation can be an effective way to reduce stress, which can be a major contributor to IBS symptoms. Meditation can help with IBS symptoms, as it has been shown to reduce symptoms such as abdominal pain, bloating, and constipation. Below is a guided meditation script that can help manage IBS symptoms. It is important to keep in mind that everyone is different and what works for one person may not work for another.

If you're looking to reduce your IBS symptoms, there's no better way to do it than with a meditation script. A meditation script is a way to guide yourself through a meditation practice that can help relax your body and mind, reduce stress, and reduce IBS symptoms.

Here's a simple yet effective meditation script for IBS symptom relief:

Find a comfortable position and close your eyes.

Allow your thoughts and worries to drift away.

Notice your body. Notice any tension or discomfort.

Focus on your breath and follow its rhythm.

Imagine that you're breathing in healing energy and breathing out any discomfort or pain. Take slow, deep breaths. Imagine that the breath is a healing balm, soothing your body and relieving any tension.

Continue to focus on your breath and the healing energy moving through your body. On each exhale, relax a little more deeply. Healing energy enters your body, soothes your digestive system, and calms down any IBS-related symptoms.

Take slow, deep breaths and imagine that each inhalation brings in healing energy and each exhalation releases any discomfort or pain. Focus on taking slow, deep breaths while picturing a healing balm soothing your body and relieving any tension.

Visualize a warm, healing light pouring into your body and melting away any discomfort or pain. Imagine the energy entering your body and calming IBS-related symptoms. Allow the light to gently bring a sense of peace and relaxation, making your body feel lighter and more at ease.

By taking the time to focus on your breath and visualize a calming place, you can help to relax your body and mind and reduce IBS symptoms, allowing you to find relief. Regularly practicing this meditation can also help to reduce stress and keep your IBS symptoms at bay.

Chapter 31

Meditation for Constipation Relief

Meditation is an effective and natural way to relieve constipation and promote regular bowel movements. It can help you relax, reduce stress, and increase your awareness of your body and its needs. By using a guided meditation script, you can target the physical and mental causes of constipation while also calming your mind.

This script can help you relax and clear your mind, allowing your body to relax and focus on its natural processes.

Begin by finding a comfortable position. You may sit or lie down in whatever way is most comfortable for you.

Close your eyes and take deep, slow breaths. As you inhale, focus on the air going into your lungs. As you exhale, focus on the air going out. Notice the sensation of the air as it enters your body and follows its path of air back out of your body. Allow yourself to relax into the rhythm of your breathing.

Feel your abdomen as it rises and falls with each breath. Notice any tightness, tension, or discomfort. As you continue to focus on the sensation in your abdomen, imagine a wave of relaxation flowing through your body. With each breath, allow the wave to build, slowly creating a wave of relaxation and comfort throughout your body. With each breath, feel your body becoming more relaxed and your digestion becoming more efficient.

While breathing deeply, visualize a white light entering your body. Feel the warmth and comfort of this light as it travels through your body. Notice how it brings peace and relaxation with it.

When you feel completely relaxed, focus on your digestive system.

Envision your entire digestive system, from your stomach all the way down to your intestines. Visualize the muscles working together to push the food down the digestive tract. Imagine that your digestive system is working to its fullest potential, allowing for the maximum absorption of nutrients. Visualize the waste in your body being flushed away.

Now, bring your awareness to any blockages or tightness in your abdomen. As you breathe, imagine the tightness melting away, allowing the relaxation wave to move through your abdomen more freely. Continue to imagine the wave of relaxation moving through your abdomen until it reaches the area of your colon.

MEDITATION FOR CONSTIPATION RELIEF

Notice any tightness or discomfort in the area of your colon.

Again, imagine the wave of relaxation moving through the area, allowing the tightness to release. Continue to focus on the wave of relaxation as it travels through your abdomen and colon. Allow the wave of relaxation to continue to move through your body, relaxing any other areas of tension.

Now, focus on the part of your digestive system that is blocked. Picture the food being stuck and unable to move. Visualize it slowly melting away, and the blockage being released.

Feel the relief and relaxation as the blockage is cleared.

Continue to take deep, slow breaths while visualizing the process of your digestive system working normally. Feel the tension and stress melting away and the energy flowing freely through your body.

Finally, with each breath, imagine the wave of relaxation spreading to your entire body, allowing it to relax deeply.

Take a few moments to sit in stillness, noticing the sensations in your body and the feelings of relaxation and comfort that linger.

When you are ready, slowly open your eyes and return to the present moment.

By using this simple meditation script for constipation relief, you can help your body naturally relax and move the food through your digestive system. By taking the time to practice this meditation script for constipation relief, you can promote healthy digestion and reduce your symptoms. With regular meditation practice, you will notice lasting improvements in your digestive health.

Chapter 32

Meditation to Help Your Child Get Out of Fight or Flight

Meditation can help children become more aware of their emotions and surroundings, and can also help reduce stress and anxiety. Meditation is a wonderful way to help children relax and find peace of mind. It can help them develop a healthy sense of self-awareness and self-regulation, as well as cultivate an attitude of acceptance and understanding.

As parents, it's important to equip our children with the tools they need to manage their stress and emotions. Meditation is an incredibly powerful tool for helping kids become calmer and more centered.

When our children are in a state of fight, flight, or freeze, they are in a state of heightened alertness and stress; their bodies and minds are on high alert, and they are trying to protect themselves from potential threats. In these moments, our children are in survival mode; their goal is not to feel better, but rather to protect themselves from harm.

The goal of meditation for our children is to help them transition out of this state of fight, flight, or freeze and into a more relaxed state of rest, digest, and heal. This allows them to access a more balanced and regulated state of mind and body, enabling them to better manage their emotions and respond to stressful situations in a more healthy way.

When helping our children to move out of fight, flight, or freeze, it is important to create a safe and calming environment. This can be done by providing a peaceful space in which they can relax and by speaking to them in a supportive and nurturing way. Once the environment is set, it is then important to guide our children through a meditation script that is tailored to their needs.

This guided meditation script is designed to help your child move out of fight, flight, or freeze and into a state of rest, digest, and heal. It's important to explain the process to your child, and provide them with instructions on how to do the meditation.

Start by having your child sit in a comfortable position, either cross-legged on the floor, lying on their bed, or sitting in a comfortable chair.

"Take a few moments to settle in, allowing you body to relax and your breath to become even.

Next, take a few moments to focus on your breath. Notice your breath as it moves in and out of your body. Notice the sensation of the breath, where in your body you feel your breath the most. Observe your breath as it moves in and out of your body. Now, begin to expand your awareness of your entire body. Notice any areas of tension or tightness and gently bring your attention to them.

Visualize a gentle flow of energy, like a warm liquid, melting away the tension.

As you continue to focus on your body, bring attention to your heart. Feel a sense of love and compassion for yourself. Picture a golden bubble of light surrounding your body.

Notice any thoughts or feelings that come up. These thoughts and feelings do not have to be acted upon, but simply acknowledged.

Now, imagine a safe and peaceful place. This could be a beach, a meadow, or a special spot in your house. Visualize this place in vivid detail, including what you see, feel, hear, and smell.

Once you can clearly picture your peaceful place in your mind's eye, imagine a path that you can walk on, winding its way through the beautiful scenery. This path can have any shape or direction that you choose.

As you follow the path, notice the different sensations in your body. Focus on the senses in your body until you reach the end of your path.

When you arrive at the end, take a few moments to just be in this peaceful place, breathing in the calming energy.

When you are ready, open your eyes and return to the present moment."

If needed, repeat this meditation script multiple times throughout the day.

Meditation can help our children to gain more control over their emotions, to better manage stress, and to develop healthy coping strategies for times of difficulty. By practicing this meditation regularly, your child will be better equipped to manage their emotions and stay in a state of rest, digest, and heal.

Chapter 33

Meditation to Feel Safe

Meditation is a wonderful way to relax and create a sense of safety. No matter what you're facing, meditation can bring you a sense of calm and protection from the outside world.

Find a comfortable seated position and close our eyes. Take a few moments to settle in and let go of any tension in your body.

The following script will help you do just that.

Take a few deep breaths, closing your eyes and focusing on your breath. As you inhale, notice your breath coming in, and as you exhale, notice your breath going out. With each breath, allow yourself to feel more relaxed and safe. Allow yourself to become more and more relaxed.

As you continue to focus on your breath, bring your awareness to your body as a whole. Notice any sensations that arise as you observe your body. Now, notice if any of these sensations are bringing up any feelings of fear or anxiety. Allow yourself to be with these feelings without judgment. Feel the tension slipping away and the calmness that comes with it. Allow your body and mind to become still, your thoughts become quiet, and your worries drift away.

Visualize yourself in a safe and secure place--somewhere that brings you peace. It could be a place in nature, a special spot in your home, or any other place that makes you feel secure.

Imagine yourself in that space and notice how it looks, how it feels, and what it smells like. Allow yourself to explore this safe space. Notice any details that stand out to you. Feel the warmth of the sun, feel the coolness of the breeze, and take in the views around you.

This is your safe space.

Let go of all expectations and allow yourself to be in the moment.

Allow yourself to simply be here in this safe place, free of stress and worry. Immerse yourself in the feelings of safety and security, and notice how they affect your body and mind.

Visualize yourself feeling more relaxed and at ease. Continue to take deep breaths in and out and focus on the feeling of safety. Feel the peace that comes with this feeling, and how it brings comfort to your body and mind.

Take a few moments to really appreciate the feeling of safety and security. Feel the comfort of being in a safe place and how it allows your body and mind to relax.

MEDITATION TO FEEL SAFE

Feel the safety and security that comes with knowing this place. Allow yourself to be in this space, feeling protected and secure.

Take as much time as you need to be in this safe space.

Now, imagine that a bubble of protection surrounds you.

This bubble is made up of whatever makes you feel safe and secure. It can be a physical sensation, such as a warm hug or a specific color. It can also be a spiritual presence, such as an angel or a divine being.

Once you have identified what makes you feel safe, take a few moments to imagine being surrounded by this bubble of protection. Notice how this bubble of protection creates a sense of security.

Allow yourself to relax and feel safe within this bubble. As you continue to meditate, repeat this mantra to yourself: "I am safe and secure." Each time you repeat this mantra, feel the sensation of safety and security grow within you.

When you are ready, bring your awareness back to your breath. Notice the sensation of your breath coming in and out. Take a few more deep breaths, and when you are ready, slowly open your eyes. Remember that this safe place is always there for you, and you can always return to it whenever you need to.

Chapter 34

Meditation for Connection

This meditation script is designed to help you connect with yourself and the people and places around you in a meaningful and comforting way. It can help you create a sense of belonging and connection that can help you through difficult times. In this meditation, you'll explore the powerful healing effects of being connected to others and to your environment, and how it can help you live with a greater sense of purpose and wholeness.

Begin by finding a comfortable position.

You can sit, stand, or lie down.

Close your eyes, and take a few deep breaths to ground yourself. Feel the rise and fall of your chest, the stillness in between each breath, and the expansiveness of your lungs. As you settle into this moment, notice your breath and make a conscious effort to relax your body and mind.

We'll start with a grounding exercise.

Take a moment to focus on your body. Notice the sensation of your feet on the ground, your body against the chair, or your hands in your lap. Feel the physical connection between you and the surrounding environment.

Imagine that you have roots that extend deep into the earth below. Feel the energy of the earth coming up into your body, nourishing and calming your body with each breath you take.

Now, bring your attention to your breath. Notice the sensation of your breath as it moves in and out of your body. Feel the air touching your skin as you breathe in and out.

Now, bring your attention to your heart. Imagine a bright, warm light radiating from your heart. This light is a source of connection and belonging. You can use this light to connect with yourself and the people and places around you. As you imagine this light radiating out of your heart, feel a sense of connection and belonging.

Know that you are not alone.

Now, bring your awareness to the energy of the wider world. Feel the energy that is shared between all living beings, and know that you are a part of this interconnected network of life.

You are part of this world.

You belong here.

MEDITATION FOR CONNECTION

Now, bring your awareness to the energy of the earth that supports us. Feel the stillness and quiet of the land, and know that you are a part of this great and ancient cycle of life.

Now, bring your attention back to your breath. Notice the sensation of your breath as it moves in and out of your body. Feel the air touching your skin as you breathe in and out.

When you are ready, take a few moments to open your eyes and come back to the present. Take a few deep breaths to ground yourself.

Now, take a moment to reflect on the sense of connection and belonging that you experienced during this meditation. Remember that it is always there, and that you can come back to it at any time.

Take a few moments to sit in stillness before slowly transitioning back into your day. Carry with you the feeling of belonging and connectedness that you've cultivated during this meditation.

Remember, you are not alone.

Chapter 35

Meditation for Pain Relief

If you're suffering from chronic pain, meditation can help you find relief. Studies have shown that meditation can reduce pain, decrease anxiety, and improve overall well-being. It can help to reduce the intensity of pain, reduce its duration, and even prevent it from returning.

With meditation for pain relief, the goal is to help you become more aware of the present moment, to focus on the here and now, and accept the moment as it is.

This meditation script for pain relief will help you relax and reduce your experience of pain. Take a few moments to get into a comfortable position. Some people find it helpful to sit in a chair with their feet flat on the floor. If that's not comfortable for you, you can lie down on your back.

Close your eyes and focus your attention on your breath. Notice the sensation of the air as it enters and leaves your body. Notice the rise and fall of your chest and belly with each breath.

Now, direct your attention to the area of your body where you're experiencing the pain.

Notice the sensation without trying to change it. Simply notice and accept it as it is.

Now, imagine that the pain is like a wave. Allow it to come and go, without pushing against it. As you do this, visualize warm, healing energy traveling to the painful area.

Imagine that it is soothing and calming the pain.

Continue to observe the pain without judgment. Allow yourself to accept it without resistance.

As you continue to relax, let go of any thoughts and emotions that are associated with the pain.

Release any tension in your body and allow yourself to relax deeper.

Imagine a soft, warm light radiating from any remaining areas of pain. Picture the light as a balm, gently soothing the area and allowing it to relax. As the light continues to expand, allow it to spread throughout the body.

Now, imagine the sensation of the pain dissipating, slowly and gradually.

Visualize the pain slowly melting away and being replaced by a sensation of relaxation.

Continue to focus on your breath and imagine the pain slowly disappearing. Notice how the area of pain is becoming lighter and more relaxed with each breath.

Now, imagine a wave of relaxation washing over your entire body, calming every cell and muscle. Allow the wave to wash away any tension and stress.

Imagine that the pain is slowly fading away, replaced with a sense of well-being and inner peace. Allow yourself to relax more deeply and to enjoy the feeling of peace and relaxation.

Now, let's move on to visualizing a comfortable and safe place. Imagine a place where you feel secure and relaxed. It can be a favorite spot in nature or a place you have only visited in your dreams. As you relax into this space, imagine the pain and tension fading away.

Allow yourself to let go and experience a deep sense of peace and relaxation. As you do, if you notice any negative thoughts or feelings, simply acknowledge them and let them pass.

Take some time to stay in this state of relaxation and peace.

Finally, take a few moments to bring your awareness back to the present moment. Notice the sounds in the room, the sensations in your body, and the stillness inside you.

When you're ready, slowly open your eyes and come back to the room. Take with you the sense of relaxation and peace that you've cultivated.

Whenever you need pain relief, you can use this meditation script. You can practice it anywhere and anytime. You can practice it for a few minutes or for a longer period. By using this meditation script for pain relief, you can find relief from your chronic pain and bring more peace and relaxation into your life.

Chapter 36

Make Meditation a Long Term Part of Healing Your Vagus Nerve

Making meditation a part of your long-term healing of your vagus nerve is one of the best ways to keep your body and mind in balance. By taking the time to sit in stillness and practice meditation, you can give your body the rest and relaxation it needs to function optimally.

When you practice meditation regularly, you will see the benefits it has on your vagus nerve. You may experience improved digestion, better emotional regulation, and a reduction in stress and anxiety. As your practice grows, you find that the benefits of meditation become more profound.

Meditation is an ancient practice that has been used for centuries to bring peace and healing to people's lives. It is a powerful way to bring balance and harmony to the mind and body, reducing stress and restoring balance.

Besides the guided meditations included in this book, there are other types of meditation that can help regulate your vagus nerve, such as body scan, mantra, or visualization meditation, that you can practice on your own. You can write your own scripts, either using the ones in this book as a base or start from scratch.

There is no right or wrong way to practice meditation. Find works best for you.

Taking the time to cultivate a regular meditation practice can be a powerful act of self-care and a great way to stay balanced and healthy. Self-care is essential for the health of your vagus nerve, so make time for activities that make you feel relaxed and nurtured.

It may take some time to get used to meditating, but it's important to be patient and consistent in order to see the best results. Be kind and gentle with yourself when meditating. Don't judge yourself if your mind wanders, or if it takes time to get used to the practice. Allow yourself to be present in the moment and trust that the practice is helping you to heal your vagus nerve.

By taking the time to make meditation a part of your long-term healing of your vagus nerve, you can feel the positive effects of the practice. Meditation can have an almost immediate effect on your mental and physical health, but it may take some time for you to feel the full benefits. Don't get discouraged if you don't see results right away. Remember, meditation isn't a one-size-fits-all solution. What works for one person may not work for another. Take your time to find a practice that resonates with you and take whatever steps you need to make it part of your long-term healing plan. With consistent practice, you can feel more relaxed, more connected to your body, and more in control of your overall health and well-being.

When you practice meditation regularly, you can see the benefits it has on your vagus nerve. You may experience improved digestion, better emotional regulation, and even a reduction in stress and anxiety. As your practice grows, you find that the benefits of meditation become more profound.

Making meditation a part of your long-term healing of your vagus nerve is one of the best ways to keep your body and mind in balance. By taking the time to sit in stillness and practice meditation, you can give your body the rest and relaxation it needs to function optimally. Meditation is one of the most powerful tools we have for healing, and when it comes to healing the vagus nerve, it can be an invaluable part of a long-term healing journey.

Made in the USA
Las Vegas, NV
20 March 2024